Reminiscences

of

Justice William Sylvester White

Copyright © 1990

U.S. Naval Institute
Annapolis, Maryland

Preface

In the first few months of 1944, 16 black enlisted men went through officer training at Great Lakes, Illinois. Of the group, 12 were commissioned as ensigns and one as a warrant officer. They were the Navy's first black officers. Collectively, the group has come to be known as the Golden Thirteen. In the autumn of 1986, the Naval Institute began an oral history project involving the eight surviving members of the group. This volume represents the life story of one of those eight men, Justice William Sylvester White.

Justice White was one of several members of the Golden Thirteen who grew up in the Chicago area, and he has lived there much of his life. In the years following his graduation from law school in 1937, White began his legal career working for lawyers in Chicago. Then he became the token black in the U.S. attorney's office in Chicago, representing the interests of the federal government. He was in that job when World War II got under way, and he subsequently enlisted in the Navy in 1943. As soon as he had completed recruit training at Great Lakes, he was put into the officer training program that led to the commissioning of the Golden Thirteen.

During his time as a commissioned officer, White served as a public information officer to get news media coverage for the achievements of black Navy men in various theaters of World War II. He also accompanied Lester Granger, a special assistant to the Secretary of the Navy, on a trip to bases in the Pacific to assess the role of black Navy men in the war effort. Following the war he resumed his legal career and later served in the cabinet of Illinois Governor Otto Kerner. Still later he became a judge and eventually attained the position of associate justice on Illinois's Appellate Court, one step below the Illinois State Supreme Court.

Justice White is a thoughtful, analytical man, given to viewing issues in broad perspectives. He brings those qualities to this oral history--along with a sense of humor that sometimes has a bite to accompany the wit. In looking at the achievements of the Golden Thirteen, he expresses a sense of pride but also the caution that it was circumstance, as much as anything, that singled out these men for a place as trailblazers. He insists that there were many, many other black men who were also capable of being commissioned.

In the transcript that follows, both the interviewer and interviewee have done some editing in the interests of clarity, accuracy, and brevity. Some sections have been rearranged to put them into chronological sequence. The original verbatim transcript is on file with the Naval Institute. The transcription was done by Ms. Deborah Reid and Ms. Joanne Patmore of the Naval Institute's oral history staff.

                                                Paul Stillwell
                                                Director of Oral History
                                                U.S. Naval Institute
                                                February 1990

WILLIAM SYLVESTER WHITE

Birthplace

Chicago, Illinois, 27 July 1914

Education

Hyde Park High School, Chicago, Illinois, graduated 1931
University of Chicago, A.B., 1935
University of Chicago Law School, J.D., 1937

Military Service

1943:   Navy recruit training at Great Lakes, Illinois
1944:   Officer candidate training, Great Lakes, Illinois
1944-1945: Public information officer, Great Lakes Naval Training Station/Ninth Naval District, Great Lakes, Illinois
1945-1946: Public information officer, Navy Department, Washington, D.C.

Professional Experience

1939-1943, 1946-1954: Assistant United States Attorney, Northern District of Illinois
1954-1955: Assistant State's Attorney, Cook County, Illinois
1955-1961: Deputy Commissioner of the Department of Investigation of the City of Chicago
1961-1964: Director of the Department of Registration and Education of the State of Illinois; chairman of the Board of Vocational Education and Vocational Rehabilitation of the State of Illinois; chairman of the Board of Natural Resources of the State of Illinois
1964-1980: Judge of the Circuit Court of Cook County, State of Illinois
1980-present: Justice of the Illinois Appellate Court

Professional Organizations

National Council of Juvenile and Family Court Judges, national president, 1978-1979
Commission on Accreditation, American Correctional Association, commissioner, 1983-1988
State of Illinois Commission on Children, member
Illinois Commission on Delinquency Prevention, commissioner
Chicago-Cook County Criminal Justice Commission, commissioner
Juvenile Problems Committee, Judicial Conference of the Illinois Supreme Court, member
International Juvenile Officers Association, member

Civic Organizations

Boy Scouts of America, Executive Board of Chicago Council
National Conference of Christians and Jews
National Association for the Advancement of Colored People
Chicago Urban League

Publications

With Professor Jill J. McNulty, Chapter I, titled, "The Concept of Juvenile Justice in Illinois," <u>Juvenile Practice Handbook</u>, published by the Institute for Continuing Legal Education of the Illinois State Bar Association, 1974

Article entitled "The Role of the Juvenile Court Judge in the Dispositional Hearing," <u>Juvenile Court Newsletter</u>, Vol. IV, No. 1, April 1974, published by the National Council of Juvenile Court Judges

With Professor Jill K. McNulty, article titled, "The Juvenile's Right to Treatment: Panacea or Pandora's Box?," published in the <u>Santa Clara Law Review</u>, Vol. 16, No. 4, 1976

"Statement of William S. White," published in the <u>Pepperdine Law Review</u>, Vol. 6, No. 3, 1979

Article titled, "Are Juvenile Courts Doing the Job?," <u>UPDATE on Law-Related Education</u>, Vol. 3, No. 1, spring 1979, published by the American Bar Association Committee

Article titled, "Debunking Three Myths About America's Children and the Courts That Serve Them," <u>Juvenile and Family Court Journal</u>, Vol. 30, No. 3, August 1979, published by the National Council of Juvenile and Family Court Judges

Awards

Distinguished First Award, American Negro Emancipation Centennial Commission of Illinois, 1973
Good American Award, The Chicago Committee of One Hundred, 1967
Judge of the Year Award, Cook County Bar Association, 1972
Outstanding Service in the Juvenile Delinquency Field Award, John Howard Association, 1972
Hannah G. Solomon Award, National Council of Jewish Women, Area Fourteen, 1978

Authorization

The U.S. Naval Institute is hereby authorized to make available to libraries and other repositories of its choosing the transcripts of two oral history interviews concerning the life and career of Justice William S. White. The two interviews were recorded on 6 October 1986 and 22 July 1988 in collaboration with Mr. Paul Stillwell for the U.S. Naval Institute.

The undersigned does hereby release and assign to the U.S. Naval Institute all right, title, restrictions, and interest in the interviews. The copyright in both the oral and transcribed versions shall be the sole property of the U.S. Naval Institute. The tape recordings of the interviews are and will remain the property of the U.S. Naval Institute.

Signed and sealed this 26th day of January 1990.

William S. White
Justice William S. White

White #1 - 1

Interview Number 1 with Justice William S. White,
    Illinois Appellate Court

Place: Justice White's chambers, Richard J. Daley Center,
                                    Chicago, Illinois
Date: Monday, 6 October 1986
Interviewer: Paul Stillwell

Q: Justice White, to begin at the beginning, could you tell me something about your family background and your early years growing up?

Justice White: Very easy. I was born in Chicago, Illinois, on July 27, 1914. I attended the public schools in Chicago, going to James McCosh Grammar School and Hyde Park High School. Then I went to the University of Chicago, getting my A.B. degree in 1935 and my J.D. from law school in 1937.

Q: What can you say about your parents' backgrounds?

Justice White: My father was a chemist and a pharmacist, a graduate of Fisk University and the University of Illinois.* My mother was a public school teacher, a graduate of Fisk University and the University of Chicago. I am an only child.

---
*Fisk University, Nashville, Tennessee, was founded in 1866; it is a traditionally black institution.

Q: How would you describe your academic career as you came along? Obviously you did well in a lot of things to have achieved the law degree and so forth. What were some of your strengths in school?

Justice White: I don't know. I wish I could tell you. I did not have any extraordinary strengths in anything. Very average.

Q: What did you do in the way of hobbies or leisure-time activities while you were in school?

Justice White: In high school I ran on the track team, and I played soccer one season, getting my letters in both sports.

Q: To what extent did the Depression affect your family? It would take some sort of resources to get into college and then law school during that period.

Justice White: Sure. Thank goodness that my mother was a public school teacher, because my dad's business as a pharmacist plummeted.

Q: Did they provide the backing or did you get a

scholarship? How did that work to get into college?

Justice White: I wish I could say yes, I did get a scholarship, but no, I did not. They sacrificed and sent their only child to college and law school. Of course, my father violated the child labor laws by making me work in his drugstore.

Q: One thing that Admiral Gravely said of his own father was that he had imparted the work ethic to him very early in life.* Did that happen to you also?

Justice White: Not by preachment, but by example, yes. You wake up in the morning and you go to work. There was no thought of anything else.

Q: That would have been apparent also in bringing you into the family business. Was he demanding in what he asked you to do in the store?

Justice White: No. There was work to be done, and what you could do, you did. I knew that I, as a child, was not expected to do as much as a grown person, but I was expected to do as much as a kid could do.
_____
*Vice Admiral Samuel L. Gravely, Jr., USN (Ret.), has been interviewed as part of the Naval Institute's oral history program. In June 1971, he became the U.S. Navy's first black flag officer.

White #1 - 4

Q: How did you get headed toward a course in the law?

Justice White: I know you're going to say I couldn't stand the sight of blood, aren't you?*

Q: No, I'm asking you.

Justice White: I believe early on I found that law depended more on the powers of reasoning rather than memorization. I fancied medicine was a field where you called a certain bone a tibia and another one the fibula-- not for any reason, but you have to remember that's what it's called. I thought that in medicine there was a lot of memorization. My father did not encourage me to be a chemist or to be a pharmacist, and right now I don't know why he didn't. I used to be the licensing officer for this state, and as such I licensed all the professions, including pharmacy.** I used to tell the pharmacists that my father didn't think I had the intellect to become a pharmacist, so he sent me into law. I'll bet that pleased them.

---

*The reference to blood is Justice White's sardonic way of indicating that medicine and law were among the few career choices available for black professionals in the 1930s.
**From 1961 to 1964, Justice White was Director of the Department of Registration and Education of the State of Illinois.

Q: It seems to me that a good deal of memorization is required in the law also.

Justice White: Well, there is some. For example, there are some justices who sit here with me who can not only remember the case, but the citation, on what side of the page a circled quotation can be found. I don't have that capacity.

Q: Did it appeal to you because of the challenge it would impose on analytical thinking and using your mind?

Justice White: I think so.

Q: Were there any role models or examples that you followed in going into the law?

Justice White: Of course, I came along where I would read the exploits of somebody like Clarence Darrow.* Then, too, there were legendary giants here in the black community, like one who died recently, Earl B. Dickerson,

---

*Clarence S. Darrow (1857-1938) was an American lawyer who practiced in Chicago from 1888 onward. He was the defense counsel in the 1924 murder trial of Nathan Leopold and Richard Loeb and in the 1925 "monkey trial" of John T. Scopes, who was charged with violating a Tennessee law against the teaching of evolution.

for whom I later went to work.* Then there were some guys who came down the pike just ahead of me.

For example, one who is now dead, his father worked for the Board of Health as a bacteriologist. My dad worked as a chemist in that same Board of Health. And he was about three years ahead of me, so he was always ahead of me in school and did quite well. Indeed, his father would always bring his son's report cards home, and my dad would look at them, come home, and give me hell because mine weren't as good.

Q: Did you feel a desire to do well in both undergraduate and law school to please your parents?

Justice White: Of course I wanted to please my parents, yes, and I wanted to be something myself, too. I knew that the opportunity to go to school was a precious opportunity which should not be wasted. Civil servants and small business people don't live so high on the hog that they don't know that a chance to go to school is precious. My father used to tell me that his mother told him that almost anything you get, the white folks can take away from you, except learning.

---
*Earl B. Dickerson died 31 August 1986 at the age of 95. He served as an Army officer in World War I and later organized the first American Legion post for black veterans in Chicago. Among Dickerson's many accomplishments, he was chief executive officer of the Supreme Life Insurance Company and a 30-year board member of the NAACP.

White #1 - 7

Q: Did you feel a sense of motivation, then, that was more internal than external?

Justice White: I don't know.

I went to James McCosh Grammar School, which is at 65th and Champlain. I lived at 63rd and Eberhart. Then I went to Hyde Park High School, which was at 63rd and Stony Island. Then I went to the University of Chicago, which was at 58th and University. All of them involved walking east from home something less than two miles to get to school. So every time I made a step, it seemed to me it was the next logical thing. The high school where I attended, a good portion of the kids were leaving and going to the University of Chicago. A good portion of the people who were with me in undergraduate school were going to law school. So I never regarded anything as a giant step; it was just the next logical thing.

Q: What were the job prospects when you got out of law school?

Justice White: Then reality hit. I graduated from law school when I was 22, small of stature, and black. So there was no thought of me earning a living except on a governmental job or earning a living out of the black community. I got out in 1937. Although we had had four years of Roosevelt, there was still a Depression.*

I first set up shop where I acted as law clerk, really, for a very successful criminal lawyer, Joseph Clayton, a marvelous lawyer.** He had his office in a rundown building in the ghetto on Chicago's south side. The toilet was down the hall and was not locked, and it was dirty. It wasn't really the kind of life I wanted.

An opportunity came for me to join one of the few black attorneys who had an office in the Loop, so I left Clayton, and I came downtown, and I officed with Earl B. Dickerson.

Somewhere along the line, there was a gap in my practice of law for about six months just before my mother died, and I worked as a case worker for the relief organization. I got enough money to buy a couple of new suits, a secondhand car, and I was in business again. So I quit that and went back to the practice of law, into the office of Earl B. Dickerson. I wasn't making any money.

[At this point, out of range of the tape recorder, Justice White showed the interviewer a photograph on his office

---

*Franklin D. Roosevelt was President of the United States from March 1933 until his death in April 1945. His administration initiated a wide variety of Depression relief measures as part of its "New Deal."
**Joseph E. Clayton, Jr.

wall. The photo was taken in a room when White, in his uniform as a Naval Reserve ensign, was with his wife and father. In the room was a window lettered with White's name and the fact that he was an attorney.]

Q: What building was the window in?

Justice White: It was in our apartment. We lived in a first-floor apartment of a two-apartment building.

Q: Was that the first time you hung out your shingle, figuratively?

Justice White: Yes. But simultaneously I also had it in the offices I have spoken of. If there was a chance of picking up business in the neighborhood, I wanted to do that.

Q: What year was that?

Justice White: Nineteen thirty-seven. I remember telling my mother, "I'm a lawyer. I can't be out here washing windows."

She said, "When you earn enough money so that you can pay somebody to do it, you won't have to do it anymore." So from little things like that, I guess, I learned the work ethic, but nobody sat down and said, "Now this is the way the Puritans and the Pilgrims believed."

Q: What sort of cases were involved when you worked for Mr. Dickerson?

Justice White: He was general counsel for a black insurance company. I didn't get to court as often with him as I did when I was with Clayton, because Joe Clayton was a trial lawyer, and at least I would appear on motions and whatnot for Joe Clayton. But with Dickerson I did not get to court often.

Don't get the impression that all of this covered a long period of time, because it covered only two years. I got out of school in '37, and in 1939 a friend of mine who had gone both to Hyde Park High School and to the University of Chicago asked me how I would like to be an assistant United States attorney. I said, "I'd like it very much. I'd like to be a United States senator. I'd like to be President of the United States. What else is new?"

He said, "No, no kidding." He was one of the guys who grew up in the neighborhood with me. It developed that he had worked with a man who was about to be appointed the United States attorney, and he was going to clean the office and put in new people. He asked this friend of

White #1 - 11

mine, Charles Browning, I guess, to suggest who should be the token black. Almost everything good that has happened to me since then has happened as the result of that chance conversation I had with Charles Browning. I was appointed assistant United States attorney, and it was from that position that I entered the Navy.

Q: Was it a practice then to have the token black, or was this the first time?

Justice White: No. I was not a first.

Q: Was it something that came in with the Roosevelt Administration?

Justice White: No, I think not. I think they had had token blacks before, under the Republicans.

Q: What was involved in your work in that office?

Justice White: I tried some criminal cases, but basically I was on the civil side of the office, handling contracts and tort cases, regulatory cases for the government.

Q: Do you have any examples you might cite, some that particularly stand out?

Justice White: Once, many years later, when I was putting my name in the ring to be a judge, they asked me to name some appeals cases that I had. The only cases I could recall were the cases that I lost.

There was a case of some kids who went through a hole in the perimeter fence around Fort Sheridan--and then scaled a six-foot fence, which was not topped by barbed wire, and found some grenades.* These were pretty big kids. They then went to their homes in Lake Forest and buried these grenades in a vacant lot. Along came some little kids who found them. They were horribly disfigured because they detonated these things. I don't even remember the name of it; it's not important.

No great history was made, but it involved the question, as you can see from what I said, of proximate causation. What was the negligence of the United States Government when these things were well within Sheridan, surrounded by two fences, and didn't the trespass committed by the teenagers insulate the government from any liability anyhow? But I couldn't sell it. You had these poor little kids all messed up, and the judge found for the plaintiffs.

Another case. I won this one. I was almost ashamed to win it. There was a flood, and the government urgently

---
*Fort Sheridan is a U.S. Army post on the shore of Lake Michigan. It is north of Chicago and a few miles south of the Great Lakes Naval Training Center.

needed housing accommodations built. An experienced contractor and builder got the contract. He needed financing, so he went to a local bank and got financing. This bank had him sign a note, took back a trust receipt on the product as it was made. Although it was redundant, they might have had mortgages. The banker tied him up every way you could have possibly imagined.

The man did perform his job; he made the merchandise. The banker was told the merchandise had been completed, and the government was aware of his interest as a lien holder. But the poor manufacturer owed income tax, so before Uncle Sam paid the manufacturer for making the things, Uncle Sam with the other hand took it back, saying, "Oh, no, you don't get it because you owe taxes." I think I was arguing that case just before I went into the service. That banker sees me yet and talks about that case, because he fancied himself quite an expert on secure transactions.

Q: So you were defending the interest of the government to make sure the tax money was paid?

Justice White: Yes, yes.

One other case, I wasn't too proud of this one either. It was one of the few criminal cases I tried. Some nuts used to go out in Washington Park and make inflammatory speeches. Nobody paid them much attention. Along came the war, and these nuts were saying, "When Tojo comes, we blacks will join Tojo."* That was the name of the Japanese prime minister. What should have happened, a guy with a club should have gone there and hit them and driven them out of the park. But no, during the war hysteria, we prosecuted them for sedition. It was seditious. Of course, we convicted them. That was one of the last criminal cases I tried before I went into the service.

Q: How does that go against the right of free speech? Is it different when you make that kind of a statement?

Justice White: I guess sedition can only be committed at times of war, so, I guess, in a sense, we have free speech, but, as Holmes said, you can't holler "Fire!" in a crowded theater.** I guess with that same philosophy, you cannot be, by words, aiding the enemy.

Q: As the token black, did you have equal status with other people of your rank in the U.S. attorney's office?

Justice White: Yes. I think they thought it was safer to have me handling civil rather than criminal cases most of

---
*Lieutenant General Hideki Tojo (1885-1948) was a Japanese Army officer who served as his country's Minister of War, 1940-41, and Prime Minister, 1941-44. He was eventually hanged as a war criminal.
**Oliver Wendell Holmes (1841-1935) was an associate justice of the U.S. Supreme Court from 1902 to 1932.

the time. Because of that, I think my chances of becoming a supervisor in that office were probably minimal, but I enjoyed it. I didn't concentrate on the hole; I concentrated on the doughnut.

Q: Why would it make a difference, civil versus criminal?

Justice White: In the first place, a criminal case would likely be a jury case, and a jury selected in those days in the northern district of Illinois would be predominantly white. There might have been some thought that I would not be able to convince a white jury to sentence a white man for breaking the law. I doubt if that were true, but there might have been that thought.

Q: What steps led to you joining the Navy?

Justice White: I wish I could say that right after Pearl Harbor I went down and knocked on the door and said, "I want to get into the Navy right now." But I did not do that. Indeed, I had kind of thought that my work with the Department of Justice was almost as important as that of FBI men, and I felt perhaps that it might be of some interest to my draft board that I was working for the United States Department of Justice.

Q: Were FBI men exempt at that time?

Justice White: Yes, they were. I had already asked to get into the FBI, too, but at that time Mr. Hoover was not permitting blacks to get into the FBI.* It used to disgust me that whenever they had some undercover work to do, they would take on a smart black detective and have him work with them, thereby eliminating the necessity of having black agents.

Q: They would get somebody from the local police force?

Justice White: Yes. What was your question?

Q: How you got into the Navy. Did you have active dealings with the draft board on this?

Justice White: Yes. I had a friend who was in the Navy. A close enough friend I was best man at his wedding.

Q: Who was he?

---

*J. Edgar Hoover (1895-1972) was director of the Federal Bureau of Investigation from 1924 to 1972. He was noted for his antipathy to blacks, including Martin Luther King.

Justice White: Lewis Reginald Williams.* He was telling me about the service opportunities. He was in the selection office at Great Lakes, so he said, "You ought to do well on the tests that they give you, and that ought to give you the preferment of getting into the service school of your choice."**

Q: Had the Navy by that time dropped the restriction that blacks could be stewards only?

Justice White: Yes. This fellow I'm speaking of was one of the first blacks admitted into the Navy under the new policy that permitted them to be assigned to general service rather than as cooks and servants.*** Incidentally, the very press announcement that Knox put out included something like, "We're going to take Negroes in for general service, but there is no present intention of commissioning

---
*Williams was one of the 16 black enlisted men selected to undergo officer training at Great Lakes, Illinois, in early 1944. Of the 16, Williams and two others did not become officers.
**Great Lakes, Illinois, a town on the shore of Lake Michigan, north of Chicago, was the site of a large naval training station that included recruit training and a number of other schools. It is now known as Great Lakes Naval Training Center.
***The change that permitted entry by black enlisted men into the Navy's general service ratings became effective in June 1942.

any of them."* They didn't just leave it open; they said, "There is no intention presently of commissioning any of them." So that was still the existing policy when I went in, although I think I felt that the Navy could not go on that way, even though that's what they said at first.

Q: Did you examine the other services as possible options?

Justice White: No, I didn't. I knew this, though. I was in Army ROTC in high school.** I didn't particularly like that, so I guess that was the reason. So when I came through selective service, I told them that I wanted to go to the Navy. A guy in the Marines, despite my size, expressed some interest, and it was really flattering. For a while I wavered. I said, "No, I'd better go into the Navy and then go to Great Lakes, and my friend Mummy Williams can get me into a good service school." As I mentioned before, Mummy was in the selection office.

When I went through boots, becoming a quartermaster really intrigued me, not so much that I wanted to become a

---

*Frank Knox (1874-1944) ran unsuccessfully for Vice President of the United States in 1936. He was publisher of the Chicago Daily News when made Secretary of the Navy in 1940. Knox died in office 28 April 1944, just over a month after the Golden Thirteen were commissioned.
**ROTC--reserve officer training corps.

quartermaster rather than an officer.* But I don't know, I really wanted to be a quartermaster.

Q: But you took the overt action of going into the Navy rather than taking your chances on the draft.

Justice White: Yes, I guess that's true. I was about one step ahead of the draft board. I called up and I said, "When am I likely to be called?"

They said, "Haven't we called you yet?"

I said, "Oh!"

Q: When did you enlist?

Justice White: It must have been October '43.

Q: Did you by then have a family?

Justice White: No. I was married, but I did not have a family. I had married in '39.**

Q: So that would not have particularly helped you with the draft board, since you didn't have children.

---
*Navy recruit training has traditionally been known as "boot camp" or "boots." The newly enlisted recruits themselves are also known as "boots."
**His wife's maiden name was George Vivian Bridgeforth.

Justice White: No. Of course, they kept me pent up there at boot training and then let me out on leave, and I became a father. I became a father of twins, so the Navy chow really does something for you.*

Q: We used to hear rumors of quite the opposite when we were at Great Lakes.

Justice White: I had evidence to the contrary.

Q: Boot camp is not a fun experience for the people going through it of any race. Did you receive any harsher treatment than the white sailors, do you think?

Justice White: It was my first experience with enforced segregation. Growing up there in Chicago, I knew that white folks live over here and black folks live over here.

Q: Were you in Camp Robert Smalls then?**

Justice White: Yes. Even before you got to Robert Smalls, when you were over on the main side, they segregated the

---

*Carolyn and Marilyn White were born 28 December 1944.
**Within the Great Lakes Naval Training Station, Camp Robert Smalls was the site of training for black recruits. It was named for an escaped slave who captured the Confederate steamer Planter during the Civil War and turned her over to the U.S. Navy. He served as pilot of the Planter and later of the gunboat Keokuk.

incoming recruits to black recruits and white recruits. I remember we were marching down to the chow hall, and they had a double-level chow hall. All the white recruits were marched upstairs, and the black recruits were marched down in the basement. That hit me. But I was an aware person. I was quite mature. I had been a lawyer for many years by the time I went into the service. I had read the press release that Knox had put out, and I knew what I was in for.

Q: Can you describe the training you received? What was the routine as far as class work, marching, and whatever else you did?

Justice White: I enjoyed boot training. It sounds crazy, but I did. And I don't think I'm looking at it through rose-colored glasses, either, because of the distance now from that period. We had a chief petty officer by the name of Robinson, a white guy from Milwaukee. And the barracks were warm and comfortable. The barracks at Smalls looked like the barracks at every other camp up there. Everything looked about the same.

It was kind of a world by itself. I guess camps are still pretty nearly self-contained units with their own barber shop, with their own drill hall, rather than being for all of Great Lakes. It, to some extent, followed the pattern of the outside world, in that blacks did play on the Great Lakes football team, because in those days there were a few blacks playing on college football teams. It sounds ridiculous now, but blacks could not play on the Great Lakes basketball team. You wonder now how they could get ten white guys who knew how to play basketball, don't you? But they did.

Q: Did Chief Robinson seem comfortable to you? Do you think the Navy made a deliberate effort to pick somebody who would work well with blacks?

Justice White: Sure, I think they did.

Q: I think that the fact that he was from Milwaukee rather than from the South might well have been deliberate.

Justice White: Yes, I think so.

Q: What do you remember of the things covered in course work at boot camp?

Justice White: Once again, I remember the things I had difficulty with. I remember at the selection office they gave us two tests. One was an IQ test, and the other was a mechanical aptitude test. The mechanical aptitude test was to illustrate what you were supposed to do. They had a screw and, among other instruments, a screwdriver, and you were supposed to select the instrument. After you passed that illustration, there wasn't anything I knew. So on mechanical aptitude I was horrible, but I knocked the hell out of the other one, as I should have.

I remembered how to drill, because right out of boots they put me in officer candidate school. All the rest of the guys had been in the Navy longer. I was the most recent admittee to the Navy to be in the officer candidate school. When I was selected as recruit company commander of our company, with my ROTC experience, I knew how to drill.

Q: Was that selection made on the basis of your ROTC experience?

Justice White: I don't know why, and I don't know how either, right now. All I can remember is that in those days we had two platoons in a recruit company, and I was happy I had two assistants in charge of each platoon, and each of them was a big guy, so I didn't have any discipline problems.

Q: Did you adjust well to the regimentation that comes with Navy life?

Justice White: Sure. As I said, I was prepared for it. They asked me about the Navy chow, and I said, "Well, it's better than some of these cheap restaurants I've been eating in."

I did not like the process of getting people up in the morning. They used to come in the barracks and turn on the lights and some guy would holler, "All right, every living ass, hit the deck!" I didn't like that. Did they do like that to you for boot training?

Q: Worse than that.

Justice White: I didn't like to be disturbed that way or wake up that way, and I hated it so much that I would get up before that. When were they waking us up at what time-- at 4:30, 5:00 o'clock? Whatever time it was, I'd wake up before, so then I could have the toilet to myself, and so when that rude awakening would come along, I was already up and half-dressed.

Q: Did you have some sort of mental alarm clock?

Justice White: I don't know how I did that. I'm pretty good, though, at waking up when I want to.

White #1 - 25

Q: Did you find it easy to tackle the nautical portions of the curriculum?

Justice White: Oh, sure.

Q: Why did you specifically desire to be a quartermaster?

Justice White: Because he's the intellectual of the enlisted men, isn't he?

Q: That and the very technical ratings in the electronics field and so forth.

Justice White: Well, yes, yes. When you come to just seamanship, though. There was no need of my hoping to be a motor mach or in aviation or something or other; that was beyond my ken.* But something where all you had to do is learn signaling and navigation, I thought I could do that.

Q: How did the opportunity come about to go to officers' school?

Justice White: I fooled the Navy. I really think this is what happened. Remember, this is back in the days where they thought it necessary in news releases--it would say,

---
*Motor mach--motor machinist's mate.

"So and so, Negro." They'd even put that under your picture. You could be black as coal, and you'd have a cutline under the picture, "John Smith, Negro."

I was with a gang of fellows who had been in the U.S. attorney's office with me for many years, and most of us were young, and they were one by one going off to war. So I guess that was another thing. By the time it got to me, I was ready. I was overdue. That's what they told me at the draft board when I called. So in the federal building there was a press office. Since I was down there for many years, I knew all the guys of the press. I called up Bob Lougran, a reporter for UP.* I said, "I wish you'd kind of take special effort. You are doing it regularly anyhow, but be sure you don't miss when I'm leaving for the service. Get it into the paper and say I'm going into the Navy. Remember, Bob, don't forget I'm going."

So when the time came, I called him up and said, "You can go with that press release." So by the time I hit Great Lakes, they knew that William Sylvester White, Negro, Assistant United States Attorney, was coming into the Navy. So that's how I got to be an officer.

Q: The policy had obviously changed from Mr. Knox's stated intention.

---

*UP--United Press.

Justice White: I didn't know it had changed, but, yes, I became an officer, so it did change. But I thought that some day it might change. I had no dream that it would change so quickly, that before I could get out of boot training that it would change.

Q: So you didn't take any actual quartermaster training?

Justice White: Didn't have a chance.

Q: You didn't actively seek the officer thing, other than the publicity buildup?

Justice White: There was no place to go apply. Oh, earlier I went to the officer recruitment office, where all the white guys in the U.S. attorney's office had gone. I was interviewed by a man by the name of Ensign Drips. Isn't that awful--to remember that for 50 years? Ensign Drips. Ensign Drips went through the formality of taking my application, but it was a very embarrassing situation for him. I can just recall the tension as I sat there. He seemed to be red and whatnot. I don't know what he did, but I did not become an officer through that application; I can tell you that.

Q: Where did you go for your officer training?

Justice White: I was right there at Great Lakes. All they did was set aside a barracks for one of the black companies, and they brought in some guys, some instructors. Some of them were very good. We have maintained contact with one of the white officers who was there.

Q: Who was he?

Justice White: He was then a jaygee. His name is John Dille.*

Q: You never thought of the name "Golden Thirteen?"

Justice White: No. We were referred to as "those Negro officers."

Q: So there were only 13 in the original class.

Justice White: The sad part about it is that the man who urged me to get into the Navy, Mummy Williams, was also selected as an officer candidate. He went through the training with us, and then at the very end, although he had passing grades, he was not commissioned. I don't know why,

---

*Lieutenant (junior grade) John F. Dille, Jr., USNR, was a battalion commander in the leadership structure at Camp Robert Smalls at Great Lakes in early 1944.

but he wasn't.*

Q: It sounds as if people were chosen to go through the initial training who had a very high probability of success.

Justice White: I guess. I guess. Three people did not get commissioned, and my friend was one of the three.

Q: What was included in the curriculum?

Justice White: Communications, signaling.

Q: Was there work on tactics?

Justice White: Oh, no, nothing so fancy as tactics. Navigation, I remember. Signaling, I remember. There was a thing called aptitude for the service, I remember. I don't remember the rest.

Q: Did it strike you as very demanding, or was it easily in your capability?

---

*Bernard C. Nalty, Strength for the Fight (New York: The Free Press, 1986), makes the following statement on page 192: ". . . on January 1, 1944, sixteen black enlisted men entered a segregated officer candidate school at the Great Lakes Naval Training Station. Although all of them successfully completed the course, only twelve received commissions, a purely arbitrary number adopted by the Bureau of Personnel for reasons never explained. Of the

White #1 - 30

Q: Did it strike you as very demanding, or was it easily in your capability?

Justice White: It was kind of like fighting in the dark. It was demanding, I thought. I thought they worked us pretty hard. I thought they didn't know what they were going to do with us. It seemed to me that they were trying hard to make us prepare for any eventuality. But nothing as combat oriented as tactics. I wish I could tell you what else it was.

Q: When I went through, there was included in the curriculum an idea on officer-like behavior and what have you. Was that part of it also?

Justice White: Oh, yes. They told us about that. Call out some other things that you had in your course.

Q: We had engineering, damage control, ordnance, gunnery.

Justice White: Oh, yes, we went down to the rifle range and had some gunnery, and we also went out and fired some antiaircraft piece out there. Some pilot risked his life towing a target that we shot at. Some dumbbell shot and cut the string--he was really good, wasn't he?--and down came the target.

White #1 - 31

Q: Did you get out in boats to practice maneuvering?

Justice White: No, we did not.

Q: You said they didn't have an idea what they were going to do with you. It's tough to train you for something that's that indefinite.

Justice White: Yes. You'll find out what happened to the guys.

Q: What sort of assignment did you get then when you were commissioned?

Justice White: I was made public relations officer. Why, I don't know.

Q: Well, you had already succeeded at that with your work with the UP correspondent.

Justice White: I was made public relations officer. The Navy at that time wanted to service the black--the Negro--press, so my staff and I ground out press releases for the Negro press. There was also a CBS radio show called "Men of War, brought to you by the men of the Negro regiments at

Great Lakes."* Then they eliminated the Negro regiments, so we proudly went on with our radio show "brought to you by the men of the Negro companies at Great Lakes." Then pretty soon you had no more Negro companies as the integration went on, and we had no radio show either. I was out of a job.

Q: What sorts of things did you do in that job? Did you do interviewing? Did you write scripts?

Justice White: I had some capable enlisted men who knew more about that kind of thing than I did, but I got pretty good myself. Then I had double assignment. Since public relations was a function of the admiral of the district, I had assignment both to the naval training center and also to the admiral.** So my office was in one of the Negro regiments, but I was also part of the public relations staff for the naval district. So I had a foot in both camps, which sometimes was good, except sometimes I'd have to do duty, stand duty in both capacities.

The commanding officer of the public relations office was a white lawyer by the name of White, who had gone to the University of Chicago.*** That kind of tied in nicely.

---
*CBS--Columbia Broadcasting System, a national radio network.
**Vice Admiral Arthur S. Carpender, USN, served as Commandant of the Ninth Naval District from 3 January 1944 to 22 March 1946.
***Commander Robert Q. White, USNR.

White #1 - 33

He was very fair, absolutely fair, really a gentleman. And we ran across some very excellent white officers.

Q: Was the press receptive to your efforts to get this publicity on behalf of black sailors?

Justice White: Yes, they were receptive, and we were proficient in grinding it out. I had a staff that would make good reading out of stories that really weren't all that great. And we got linage in the black press, not equal to the Army--of course not, because the Army had generals and whatnot that were black, and the Navy only had us.

Q: In the spirit of the times, it was a patriotic era, and they were looking for military stories.

Justice White: Yes, but I remember a paper in New York. In a political cartoon that characterized the Navy, it showed the Navy a proud ship going through the waves, and a towline out pulling a little rowboat. It had, under the big ship, "The Navy," and it had under the rowboat, "Negro programs." So 99% of the blacks coming through the selection process would pick the Army. They did not want the Navy, because the Navy had a history of mistreating blacks. I don't know that the Navy is yet the preferred service.

I think we did a pretty good job, and the enlisted men who worked for me later went with Fleet Hometown News and did all right. Moses Preston, the guy who took that picture of my wife and twins in our apartment, became a chief photographer in the Navy, because he stayed over after the war.

Q: Was it part of your intent to overcome the thrust of that cartoon?

Justice White: That was my duty, yes. Sure. Hell, yes, that was it. That was the whole thing.

Q: Was recruiting black sailors a deliberate by-product of your effort?

Justice White: I don't know how to answer that. I don't know how to answer that. I will say, though, I chose as my task to give recognition to the individual blacks who were achieving in the Navy and to publicize the breakthroughs in Navy policy.

For example, the first black physician that the Navy commissioned was assigned to Great Lakes before he went out to Guam. While he was in Great Lakes, he was in charge of the sick bay. This sick bay had the usual table of petty officers and men. And I put out a press release saying, "This black man has been in charge of this sick bay, over 20 petty officers, two of whom are black." That's the way the Navy wanted me to put it out. Of course, the real story is that this black man was over a group of 20, and 18 of them were white.

So what used to kick me, they wouldn't ever turn my lines around. They would just print it as I put it out. Stupid. See, I couldn't be there preaching integration; just give the facts. I was supposed to publicize black accomplishment, and it was an accomplishment that two of the people were Navy corpsmen who were black. That's all right, but the real story is that 18 were white and under this black commanding officer. But be that as it may, we thought we did a good job.

Q: Was publicizing your own story included in your efforts--that here is what one of the first 13 black officers is doing for the Navy?

Justice White: I don't know why I didn't think of that. I was already an officer. I don't think I did that. I didn't hear much from my colleagues. Several of them were put on board ship.

White #1 - 36

Q: James Hair, for example, went to USS Mason.*

Justice White: Yes, and he went further than that too. Hair is the saltiest one of the group. I can remember when he hit barracks, I hadn't seen Hair before. He was the last of the selectees to arrive, I think, in the group when we were in training at Great Lakes. He says, "I've got more salt in my socks from washing them in seawater than all the rest of you guys put together." He was an old salt.

Q: Do you have memories of any of the other 13 specifically from the training period?

Justice White: What they did?

Q: Things such as that which you recall about Hair. What qualities and characteristics do you remember of the others?

Justice White: Well, I remember this. There was a guy who had a sister. This man is now dead, so it won't hurt if I tell this story. His name was Phillip Barnes, no kin to

---
*James Edward Hair is a member of the Golden Thirteen; his oral history is in the Naval Institute collection. In 1945 he became the first black officer in the destroyer escort Mason (DE-529), a ship with an all-black enlisted crew.

Sam Barnes.* We had two Barneses in our group. Phillip Barnes had a sister that worked in the Navy Department as a messenger or something. Whatever office in the Navy Department in Washington that she was working in, she was working in that office that would get information about the progress or lack thereof of this group of blacks they had out at Great Lakes making them officers.

Everything was hush-hush. We couldn't talk to the press; nobody was supposed to know that we were in officer training. I guess in case the thing blew up, they didn't want a whole lot of trouble. Anyhow, it was kind of a silly situation. Here we were at Great Lakes. Every recruit knew those blacks over there were doing something different from everybody else. Then, too, I guess they didn't want to jump me from apprentice seaman to ensign in one jump. I couldn't even keep up with my pay. They first made me third class, and before I knew it, they made me first class. I thought, "Gee, this Navy is really all right." I guess within nine months after I started in the Navy, I was an officer.

Q: Did they make you these in the quartermaster rating?

Justice White: I think if a guy was already rated, they

---

*Phillip George Barnes and Samuel Edward Barnes were both members of the Golden Thirteen. The oral history of Samuel Barnes is in the Naval Institute collection; Phillip Barnes died before he could be interviewed.

advanced him in his rating. For example, Jesse Arbor was already a quartermaster, so they jumped him up to first class quartermaster.* Mummy was already whatever rate they give a guy in the selection office--personnel. Since I had no rate, they made me boatswain's mate.

Q: Did you have a desire to go to sea during this period when you were working at Great Lakes?

Justice White: No, I didn't. If they had started me down a different path, yes, I would have. But I was totally unequipped. I had had this officer training thing, but I didn't feel I knew enough. If they had let me go to quartermaster school, I would have wanted to go. But I didn't think I had learned enough signaling and navigation to put me aboard a ship. Maybe I did. I just wouldn't know.

Then, too, at that time they were trying this idea of all-black ships, which was a disaster. You know, an organization like the Navy doesn't make any great big boo-boos, but they made a big boo-boo in the way they did that. They sent out to all the shore installations a notice to the commanding officers, "We're thinking about commissioning a black ship. If you have any good men of these rates, refer them to us." And every commanding
_____
*Jesse Walter Arbor is a member of the Golden Thirteen. His oral history is in the Naval Institute collection.

White #1 - 39

officer who had any sense at all didn't refer his good ones. Why would he send away his good ones? All the goofballs! I won't say that Hair was one. But there were too many people who were discards when you do it that way. I would wonder about the intelligence of the naval officer who would send his best petty officer somewhere else, wouldn't you?

Q: Yes, if he had a choice.

Justice White: He was not about to do it. So the reports I heard--I wasn't aboard, and maybe Hair could give it to you firsthand. The report I heard was that that experiment was not a howling success. So therefore the Navy saw early that that wasn't the way they could do it. The Navy was very pragmatic.

Another thing that happened, they had a horrible explosion at Port Chicago.* I think it was Port Chicago.

Q: Yes, it was, the summer of '44.

---

*On the night of 17 July 1944, 320 individuals, 202 of whom were black ammunition handlers, were killed when two merchant ships, the Quinalt Victory and the E. A. Bryan, exploded while being loaded with munitions at Port Chicago, California, about 40 miles northeast of San Francisco. A number of the ammunition handlers were subsequently court-martialed because of their reluctance to go back to work. See Robert L. Allen, The Port Chicago Mutiny (New York: Warner Books, Inc., 1989).

White #1 - 40

Justice White: And blew away many a black man.

Q: That's because many black men were assigned to the ammunition-handling gangs.

Justice White: That had a chilling effect, as you can imagine. I think they put out a rule that no more than such and such a percent of any shore installation should be black. The Navy, I think--check me out on this--but I think from that and from the experience with the PC-1264 and the Mason, the Navy became integration minded, so much so that one of my enlisted men who worked under me in public relations, when he was coming back and mustering out, said, "Well, I'm coming back to the States," he was writing me, "as a part of the Navy that's much more democratic than the nation it serves." Which was a far cry from the beginning of our story, I was going down into the basement to eat, while the white boys were eating upstairs.

Q: What were the living conditions like when you were stationed at Great Lakes? Did you still live at home?

Justice White: Yes, I lived at 6300 south, that way. You've been to Great Lakes, so you know where that is. Hard by Great Lakes there is an exclusive community that used to have more millionaires than any other community in the United States. It's called Lake Forest. I had a business that was doing pretty well back in those days, and I was in the Navy, and I thought I was going to stay at Great Lakes forever. So I bought a home in Lake Forest. My wife and I had little children. As soon as the ink was dry on my deed, I got shipped out and sent to Washington.

There I was no longer officer in charge of any radio show. I was still, from a national perspective, handling the job of a Navy public information officer, but I had more general duties. There weren't enough black things from that perspective for me to be busy, so I was just one of the guys in the press section, grinding out stuff.

Q: What sorts of stories did you work on, things regarding combat actions?

Justice White: Yes. By this time, the war was either over or winding down. One of our biggest battles was against the formation of the Defense Department. We in the Navy didn't want that.

Q: No, the Army was pushing that much more, and it was also pushing for a separate Air Force.

Justice White: Yes. I even convinced people that, from a

black perspective, there should be competition among the services as to who could do the best job in the utilization of black personnel. Because everything I was doing was from the point of view of utilization, not necessarily because it's good and fair and integration, but because that's the most efficient way to use your personnel. I guess I was closer to administration than a public relations officer should be, but I was involved in it.

Q: Were you pushing actively for integration? How much were you allowed to push for it?

Justice White: I was always kind of backhanded with it.

First, let me say this. The Secretary of the Navy was Forrestal by this time, and he had picked an old Dartmouth chum, Lester Granger, who was black, to make the rounds of the shore installations that had goodly numbers of blacks, to see to what extent the Navy's integration policy was being implemented.* We first made some trips around the United States--I can't recall exactly where. I know we went to New Orleans, among other places. We visited a shore installation down that way. I'd say to the commanding officer, "Do you ever get any people here from

---

*James V. Forrestal became Secretary of the Navy on 19 May 1944, following the death of Frank Knox. Lester B. Granger, an official of the Urban League, took office in the Navy Department in March 1945 as a civilian advisor on policy toward black servicemen.

the Negro press? Do you ever release anything to the Negro press? Do you grind out stuff for the press?"

They'd give me the answer, "No, we don't send anything to the Jewish press, the German press, the Japanese press. We just send it to the general press."

"Then, too," he would say, "the only time they come over here is when they hear that something is wrong."

"Did you ever ask them to come see something right?"

"No, I don't do that."

So you go talk to the black newsmen, and they'd say, "We have a lot of things to do and a lot of places to go. If he's got something good there, I presume he'll call us and tell us so we'll take a look."

So part of my bringing these things together was trying to talk a language that would be understandable by both sides.

Q: Just to indicate that they've got a mutual interest, if they could see the other point of view.

Did you take your family with you to Washington?

Justice White: No, no. My two children had been born in 1944.

We've been talking on the basis that I was one of the first black officers in the United States Navy, but the truth is, before we were commissioned, there was another black officer in the Navy, at least one other. Shortly before I left the Navy--and the war was over--I was given an assignment to write out the story of this naval ace who downed I don't know how many Japanese planes as an aviator. I read over the information they had on him, and it seemed he was a member of a civilian flight group, and a whole bunch of them went over and joined the Navy. Apparently he was light of complexion, and he thought he was passing for white.

However, intrepid Navy intelligence found out he was truly black. But I guess so long as he kept shooting down Japanese planes, they didn't care whether he was black or white. So did I cover that story? I went to New York, to the address they gave me, and looked around and saw that this was--what we had in those days--a white neighborhood. I said, "Well, damn if I'm going to pull the cover off of him just for the sake of a story." So I might have lied and said I couldn't find him. I don't remember his name.

One of our group stayed on active duty in the Navy, and that was Nelson.* He's now deceased. A very proud man, a good-looking man, about my size. One of our instructors said that he had the capacity of strutting

---

*Dennis Denmark Nelson II eventually retired from the Navy as a lieutenant commander. He died before he could be interviewed as part of the Naval Institute's oral history program. Nelson's master's thesis was published by the Navy Department in 1948: <u>The Integration of the Negro into the United States Navy, 1776-1947, with a Brief Historical Introduction</u>.

while he was sitting down. Nelson had indomitable spirit. I saw him when I went on my tour. He was on Eniwetok, which is about 20 square miles and about two feet out of the ocean. Nelson had to be proud of something, so he was proud of his shell collection. He was in charge of training leading to advancement. That was his forte. He did that, even when he was at Great Lakes. He took illiterates and taught them to read. He was dean, as he said, of Knucklehead University, old KU.

Q: Was there a leader or leaders among the group of 13 while you were taking the training?

Justice White: I think so. I said this at his wake and nobody really disputes it. Reginald Goodwin had been in the Navy longer and was probably closer to the principal Annapolis graduate associated with the Negro program, and that was Commander Armstrong.* Because Goodwin was in longer and had the ear of the powers of the Navy, I think we depended upon him in some way to convey our thinking and our feelings to the main side, and I think he was also used by main side to convey something less than orders and commands, but the desires of main side of us. So in that

---

*Reginald Ernest Goodwin died before he could be interviewed by the Naval Institute's oral history program. Commander Daniel W. Armstrong, USNR, was officer in charge of Camp Robert Smalls. He was a 1915 Naval Academy graduate who resigned his regular commission after World War I and was recalled to active duty for World War II.

White #1 - 46

regard, he was smart. In that regard, I think he was probably a leader.

Q: Did you resent the fact that the Navy was keeping you well guarded during that training period?

Justice White: It was irritating.

Q: Was there an attempt to counteract that once you got commissioned, to put you on public show and take advantage of you?

Justice White: Yes, we knew that. Yes, we expected to be exhibits. I know I did.

Q: Were you comfortable with that role?

Justice White: Yes. Don't forget, people were fighting and dying. So who am I? If my country wants me to be an exhibit, it certainly beats dying, doesn't it?

Q: It certainly does. Do you have any overall feelings about your naval experience? Any summation?

Justice White: I said at Goodwin's wake that during the time I was in the Navy, I didn't quite appreciate his role as unofficial head of the colored, and I trust that no such

White #1 - 47

person is any longer necessary. But he had a very ticklish role to play and he, I guess, did the best he could with it. That's one thing I think.

The other thing, I wouldn't be working with the Navy now in recruitment if I didn't think, like my press person felt when he was coming back, that the Navy is more democratic than the nation it serves.

Q: Among the many accomplishments you've achieved over a lifetime, that certainly is one of those with lasting effects.

Justice White: Maybe, yes. Just think what happened. The Navy reached down into a half million men and picked 16. It could have dipped I don't know how many times and gotten 16 just as good. Not all the fellows you'll talk to will think that. I know I think so. I happened to be coming down the street at the right time, and I had the right advance publicist.

A while back, I went to a meeting of NNOA.* Whatever the initials stand for, it is in fact and in truth an organization of black naval officers. It meets annually. The Navy has been nice enough during the last several years to have us meet with them. I got hold of a

---

*NNOA--National Naval Officers Association.

White #1 - 48

young black lieutenant in the Navy. I said, "It's all right for us to get together, but we'd like to see a ship." So they arranged for us to meet aboard the Kidd, a beautiful destroyer. I don't know what the point of my story is, but I guess that was the most exciting reunion we've had, and we have them annually now. The Navy pays for us to get together. Certainly when we went aboard the Kidd, there was a whole lot of good press for the Navy.*

Q: I've seen stories from that, yes.

Justice White: It's kind of dramatic. One of us--that is, Hair--got lost from the group. We didn't know he spelled his name H-A-I-R, so none of us could find him.** He heard that we were having a reunion, read it in The New York Times, and he called up the Navy and said, "Hell, I'm surviving and you haven't asked me to come." So they had to fly him out after we had already gone to sea, and they dropped him in on a helicopter. It was a joyous reunion, so that was good. I think the Navy's done well.

I was about to say I was at this meeting, and I was

---

*From 13 to 15 April 1982, the nine surviving members of the Golden Thirteen held a reunion on board the guided missile destroyer Kidd (DDG-993) at sea in the Atlantic. See PH2 Drake White, "Golden 13 Together Again," All Hands, August 1982, pages 8-11.
**As Hair explains in his own oral history, at the time he was undergoing officer training, he was temporarily spelling his last name as H-A-R-E, and that was the spelling used on his official Navy records.

sitting at the head table. They make a big to-do of us being the Golden Thirteen. Anyhow, they put us up front, and I got a note handed to me by the waiter: "Are you the Judge White that taught at the University of Illinois-Circle Campus? I believe you taught me such and such a course. My name is so-and-so." I looked out at all these people, and I wondered who sent me this note. It turned out to be a female that I had written a letter for to get into law school because she was such a good student. She went to law school, passed the bar, and now she's a captain in the Marine Corps. I think they had a Marine battalion with some good men too. No officers. The Marines were behind the Navy when it came to commissioning. Here this little girl was a captain in the Marine Corps. It was a new day. So I've seen a lot happen all this time. Not enough, but I've seen a lot happen.

Q: Do you think that the statement that came in that letter to you after the war is still true, that the Navy is still more democratic than the society?

Justice White: I think so. For example, certainly a vice admiral is the equivalent of a president of a corporation.* I don't think General Motors, United States Steel have made the progress that the Navy has. I

───────────
*Samuel L. Gravely, mentioned earlier in this interview, retired from active duty as a vice admiral in 1980.

White #1 - 50

don't think even the government has. I don't know about that. Maybe we have congressmen and senators who are comparable. I don't know. I was down in Alabama last month and was meeting with the Supreme Court of Alabama, and one of the Supreme Court justices of Alabama was a black man. So, yes, I still think, on the whole, that the Navy is more democratic than the country it serves.

Q: Thank you.

White #2 - 51

Interview Number 2 with Justice William S. White,
Illinois Appellate Court

Place: Justice White's chambers, Richard J. Daley Center,
Chicago, Illinois

Date: Friday, 22 July 1988

Interviewer: Paul Stillwell

Q: It's a pleasure to see you again, Justice White. I know I am better prepared this time than the last, because you were the first one I interviewed before, and now I've been around the circuit and gotten more background.

I'd be interested in especially your memories of that time together in Great Lakes in early 1944. How did you get the news that this was to be for officer training?

Justice White: I was the only one of the original 16 who was in boot training. I was not out of boots when I was summoned to Camp Lawrence, which was one of the Negro camps, and told that I was wanted on the main side. And I was in what was known then as a dental company, meaning I was having extensive dental work done before being sent to a duty assignment. And that was one of the purposes of recruit training: that is, to get you mentally introduced to the Navy and get you in good physical shape.

At any rate, I think I was in sick bay as a result of having several teeth pulled, and I was ordered to the main side. And, of course, it took me a long time. When I got there, oh, a half dozen officers were there waiting for me. I cannot tell you specifically who was in the group. As I told you, I was new to the Navy, and their faces were not known to me, the faces of the officers. I believe Commander Armstrong was one of them, and I don't know who else. To my recollection they had somebody from away from Great Lakes, away from this naval district, also in the group talking to me.

I remember that they invited me in, and I stood at attention, as I had learned to do, even as a recruit. And although they talked to me for what seemed to be an interminable time, nobody told me, "At ease." So there I stood at attention. And they said in substance this: "The Navy is contemplating commissioning a small number of Negroes, and your name has been submitted as one of the potential officers."

I don't know what other preliminary information they said, but they finally got down to saying, "It was thought that you might serve in the capacity of a public relations officer." I at that time was a lawyer and had no experience in writing a newspaper or doing anything else in the way of public relations, but I, at least as a lawyer, thought I was a pretty good generalist and could do most anything that required reading and writing. And if they asked me if I thought I could do the job, I probably answered, quickly, "Yes."

But then the part of the interview I do remember is that they said, "Now the policy of the Navy regarding the utilization of Negro personnel is being attacked by some Negroes. The Negro newspapers have been particularly vigorous in their attacks upon the Navy's policy. Now if the Navy makes decisions regarding the utilization of Negroes and that decision comes under attack by Negro leaders and Negro writers in the press, would you be able, still, to carry out the Navy policy?"

I said, "Well, we are at war and men are dying in following orders. And if men can die to follow orders, I guess I can follow orders." That's about all I remember.

Q: Did you see that question as a make-or-break type thing on whether you would be accepted?

Justice White: I don't know. I don't know. It was a question I was not prepared for, but, mind you, this was 1943. I was very conscious of the fact that this is still a democracy. And I lauded their efforts to change the policy through mass pressure. But I thought my duty on the inside was to follow orders, so, although I wasn't prepared for the question, my answer was forthcoming.

Q: At the time of this interview, had Lewis Williams been chosen for officer training?

White #2 - 54

Justice White: If he had already been chosen, I'm sure he would have told me. Once again, I don't remember particularly, but we were soon advised. I don't think it was at that meeting, but I think once we were assembled, we were then told that the very existence of this officer training program was a matter of secrecy. Once again, I didn't see why, but it was easy for me to keep my mouth shut.

Q: Some of the other members of the group remember it as being a while before they were told the purpose for being there. Apparently that was not your experience.

Justice White: No, it wasn't. I'm amazed that they say that.

Q: They got some communication through Phil Barnes's sister, who was in Washington. Do you remember the nature of the information she was providing?

Justice White: I do remember she was there. It was an interesting network, wasn't it? Here was a person who was probably a messenger being able to crack Navy secrecy, at least in reference to this. But I thought her information was more in the nature of when we were going to be commissioned. That's my recollection. I know I did not rely upon that to let me know why I was being considered for a commission.

And the reason that my inclusion in the group strikes me is that the Navy took me when I had just completed my boot training and started me on another course when I had hoped to go to quartermaster school. Even while in boots--although you're under quarantine, I guess you would call it, because you have to stay in there until your boot training is over--I was permitted to come out and to talk to some members of the black press whom I knew. And maybe that was the reason they chose me to be the press officer. I don't know. It's vague to me now.

Q: What was the nature of this? To announce that you were going into officer training?

Justice White: Why did I come out and talk to them? I can't remember. But there was a press service, the ANP, Associated Negro Press, that serviced the black papers in those days, run by a friend of mine by the name of Claude Barnett.* And if I told them I was going to be an officer, I guess I had to tell them the Navy was going to commission some officers. I can't recapture that. All I can remember is reporting somewhere with my boots on, and

―――――――――
*Claude Barnett was the founder of the Associated Negro Press.

they suggested, "No, you better take your boots off when you go see him."

Q: That sort of runs counter to the notion of secrecy, then.

Justice White: Yes, it does. I do remember that thereafter we were instructed to keep our mouths shut. But why did they have me come out of boots and go to the man who ran the Associated Negro Press to talk about this? I don't know. I don't know, but I can recall that I did.

Q: What impressions do you have of Commander Armstrong from that period?

Justice White: Southern, aristocratic, egotistical, sincerely interested in advancing the status of Negroes in the Navy, according to his viewpoint. I think he was sincere when he told us that we were officers, but we should remember we were colored officers and not do all the things that white officers do. He thought by that course we would ensure the success of the program. We hated it, but I'm sure he thought it best. And I guess, in a sense, it was rather like Branch Rickey telling Jackie Robinson, who was feisty by nature, "Don't let that show, Robinson.

White #2 - 57

You're a pioneer, and that might hamper others coming along."*

Q: What were some of the things that he enumerated as things that white officers did that you wouldn't be able to do?

Justice White: Principally, going to the officers' club.

Q: Would you describe him as condescending?

Justice White: I guess that's the flip side of being aristocratic, isn't it?

Q: Yes.

How would you characterize the attitude and demeanor of the instructors in the various courses?

Justice White: I don't know how they regarded their assignment, but they were not condescending. I think most of the instructors, like teachers everywhere that are good, want the people to learn. And I don't think they ever, in

---

*Branch Rickey, the president of the Brooklyn Dodgers, in the fall of 1945 signed Jack Roosevelt Robinson, a black Army officer with a spectacular background as an athlete, to a professional baseball contract. In 1947 Robinson became the first black major league baseball player and endured a great deal of verbal abuse as a result; Rickey directed him to turn the other cheek and endure the abuse.

their demeanor, talked to us like they thought that we couldn't learn it or that they were impatient with our slowness in learning it. I never got that feeling.

Q: You described Armstrong as sincere. Would you use that same adjective for the instructors?

Justice White: We didn't have too much personal contact with them. I think so. We still lived our day-to-day lives. We got up, we shaved, we showered and so forth, and we didn't always think of this as history-making. We knew it was, but in some sense we might be more concerned with what we were going to do on liberty next weekend.

Q: Well, it must have impacted on different members of the group differently, because Mr. Cooper remembers a sense of pressure of representing, say, 10,000 black sailors.

Justice White: Oh, well, yes, we knew that. We knew that we shouldn't screw up. I don't dispute that. When he said we stayed up nights and worked in the head, is he right? Yes. Nobody wanted to be wrong.

Q: But that probably would have been true had it not been such a historic occasion also.

Justice White: I don't know, but I know we worked. I can remember them talking to each guy, asking him, "How did you get here?" And there was another commander at Hampton Institute, a white commander I'd never met.* Apparently the word went out to certain shore installations—I'm just saying "apparently"; I don't know—that they were going to pick a small number of blacks. I think they even had decided in what capacity they were going to be commissioned and used. They must have sent out word, "Send us some men who qualify." Because how else could Hampton and these other people send the men together to Great Lakes? How the Navy decided to distribute and take one from here, one from there, I don't know. Or was there any competition? I really don't know how they did it.

What was your question? I think I've forgotten where I was going.

Q: I got a little distracted, too. Well, we were talking about representing others.

Justice White: About the pressures. It is true. I don't know whether I thought of it as that dramatic or not, but

---

*Commander Edwin H. Downes, USNR, was a Naval Academy graduate who had resigned his commission, worked in the field of education, and then been recalled to active service for World War II. He was officer in charge of the Naval Training School at Hampton, Virginia. He recommended some of the enlisted men at Hampton for inclusion in this first officer training program.

down deep, although when I went into the Navy, I just did not believe that the Navy was going to go on forever with a policy of utilizing blacks but having no black officers. I just didn't believe it. Now, did I think it was going to break while I was in the Navy? I thought it would break before the war was over, but little did I believe that it would break while I was in boots.

Q: You said that the group didn't want to fail. I don't think they would have had any desire to fail, whether they were the fifth or the tenth such group.

Justice White: It's a good point, and I think there's something to that. So maybe I need to back away a little bit from what I was saying. We knew we were the first--and if we didn't know it, the commander would remind us--and we didn't want to mess up if we were the first, and what we did was important.

Q: Each man has described this cooperative effort of putting forth expertise in individual areas. How did that process come together?

Justice White: Very easy. You had Jesse Arbor, who was a quartermaster, so he was helping with signaling. I guess I was helping with Navy regs--I was a lawyer at the time--

White #2 - 61

although I don't remember myself being a whole lot more help than a guy named Goodwin who later became an officer, who is now deceased. Believe it or not, the fact that I was right out of boots, some things I had learned there were fresher in my mind than they were in the minds of those guys who had gone out earlier. I've forgotten what they were, but each guy chipped in with what he could do.

Q: Was that a process that perhaps started off informally and then became more institutionalized as the time went on, this cooperation?

Justice White: I don't know that it became all that institutionalized. Is that what you gather?

Q: At least one individual described sitting around the table at night and taking each subject in sequence, and the expert on that subject discoursing on it.

Justice White: I won't say it didn't happen. It didn't impress me if it did. And some people didn't work all that hard either. Some worked harder than others, as in any class. I knew I was low man on the totem pole since I was--well, I was high man when it came to education. I guess there was nobody there with graduate degrees but me, but as far as the Navy was concerned, I was the low man. I used to tell them, "You know Commander Armstrong. You know Commander Downes at Hampton. You've got good sponsors that put you here. I don't have anybody but Mummy, so I have to hit it."*

Q: He did have a master's degree by that time, as did Martin.

Justice White: They did? At that time?

Q: At that time. So you were among the top few.

You talked about the mundane of showering and shaving. What else do you remember about the routine of a day during that training period?

Justice White: Well, I know when we were getting down to aptitude for the service, and they sent us out to drill some recruits, assigned us to a recruit company, that was throwing me in the briar patch, because I'd just come out of boots. Then I had three years of Army ROTC in high school, so I knew I could drill them. I don't know what I got in aptitude for the service, although one of the situations I remember--marching a company of men into a drill hall, and some of the companies are already there, and you've been allotted the position between two

---

*"Mummy" is the nickname of Justice White's friend Lewis R. Williams.

companies, standing at what used to be a company front. I marched them in there nicely, until I realized I had the head of the line in the wrong direction. Now, how to get these suckers back? I don't know whether I said, "Fall out and fall back in" or not, but I remember that was a little exercise that caused me some concern. But I knew I could, and I did, drill the company. I had been the apprentice CPO in my boot company, and, as I say, I called upon my high school ROTC training.

Q: Were there other things specifically designed to test leadership and to train in that?

Justice White: I don't remember that. A lot of the guys got a low grade in aptitude for the service. I just don't know how in the hell they knew. I don't know. I don't know.

Q: Back to the routine of the day. How do you remember that going?

Justice White: As I remember, the classroom was right in the barracks where we slept.

Q: That's what others remember also.

Justice White: As I remember, there was a lot of memorization. And we would try to get nonsense words, each letter of which would represent a whole thought or a sentence in the thing we had to remember. I don't recall what, but a lot of memorization.

I don't know what the hell for, but they took us down to where they had some antiaircraft guns. I'm not sure whether it was the Chicago piano or not.*

Q: Mr. Sublett recalled both the 20-millimeter and the 40-millimeter.

Justice White: Is he talking about a machine gun?

Q: Those were both antiaircraft guns.

Justice White: Well, one thing I remember, they had us shooting a gun, the barrel of which would get hot. And I thought, "If they've got guns like this aboard ship, they're in bad shape. They ought to have some sort of cooling system." You'd shoot it just for a few minutes, it would be so hot you couldn't use it. And I never did learn whether they had guns just like that aboard ship. But I thought to myself, "They're in bad shape about that." And

---
*"Chicago piano" was a nickname for the Navy's 1.1-inch antiaircraft gun.

they took us to the rifle range too. Once again, I had had that in boot training, so in some regards, I was better off that I was right out of boots. Some of these guys had been out of boots and been sitting at desks and other things for so long that they had forgotten their boot training.

Q: What were you shooting at with the machine guns?

Justice White: A target towed by a biplane.

Q: What other opportunities were there to get out of the barracks?

Justice White: You know, I don't even remember whether we had liberty on weekends or not while we were in officer training. What did the other guys say?

Q: That seems to be a memory problem. Some specifically remember it. Some seem to feel they were incarcerated for quite a long period of time.

Justice White: You see, it blended right into boot training with me, and I can't remember.

Q: The consensus seems to be that there was some. Do you

recall being able to go home and visit your wife during that period?

Justice White: My twins were born nine months later, so yes I did. [Laughter]

Q: What month were they born?

Justice White: They were born in December of 1944.

Q: So you definitely were home.

Justice White: Yes.

Q: What about physical training and exercise during that period?

Justice White: I can't remember anybody putting us through jumping jacks and all that other thing when I was in that training. Did that happen? I mean, I don't remember any of that.

Q: Apparently, at least to some degree.

Justice White: We were so different in our physical

White #2 - 67

capacities, it seems to me I would have remembered that. I think we were required to do some swimming. I think Cooper hurt his back in some sort of swimming.

Q: Yes, he did.

Justice White: I really did not see that, but he told me later that he did. I remember that. I had trouble with swimming, and so, of course, I would remember that. I don't remember any rigorous--it was cold as the dickens up there at Great Lakes.

Q: What's the grin on your face?

Justice White: I sound like I'm not being too helpful about this, but keep trying. Maybe something will come to me.

Q: What do you remember about the blending together of the men in the group and the camaraderie that developed?

Justice White: Oh, that was good. There was no question about that. I can remember when Hair came into the barracks, and somebody knew almost everybody from somewhere, some duty station before. Everybody was greeted. Have you ever found out whatever happened to

Alves?*

Q: No, I haven't. Do you have specific memories of him from that period?

Justice White: Yes. He was different, you know. He had been to sea more than anybody else. Most of his sea experience had been in the merchant marine, I think, so, of course, we listened. He helped round out the group, although Hair lied and said, "I have more salt in my socks from washing them out at sea than all you guys put together." He claimed that his last duty station had been a shore-based one, where his duty was to give short-arm inspections to a WAVE contingent.

Q: Another individual who did not get commissioned was Pinkney.** What recollections do you have of him?

Justice White: He was a lightweight, somebody who was not going to be commissioned. We were pretty well bunched up together. That's my recollection after 40 years. And I didn't know him, never saw him before that, and I've never seen him since. Never heard of him since.

---

*Although he went all the way through officer training with the Golden Thirteen, A. Alves was not commissioned at the end of the training period.
**J. B. Pinkney.

Q: Did you have an impression or information at the time on why the three men did not get commissioned--Alves, Pinkney, and Williams?

Justice White: I thought it had been since aptitude for the service was something for which we did not hand in papers and get grades. Either I presumed or I heard that it was on the basis of aptitude for the service. And that was something also of which I would not be able to see the other person perform. For example, a man who did make it claims he was out drilling his company, and they were marching, going right into a fence. And he claimed he couldn't think of how to stop them. Finally, he yelled, "Stop, damn it! Stop!" [Laughter] He said it about himself. I don't know how he did on aptitude for the service.

Q: Was there any explanation to the rest of the group on why the three didn't make it?

Justice White: No, because we weren't all commissioned at once. I got mine a few days after the rest of them got theirs, and I don't know why. That was the reason--I think that was the reason--once again, I was in sick bay, I guess. I don't know what for this time. When the Navy photographer--I told you this story before, didn't I? When the Navy photographer came out to take the picture?

Q: No, you didn't. Arbor told me the story.

Justice White: Arbor did.

Q: He said you were missing because you were getting some more work done on your teeth.

Justice White: Then that's probably right. Caused me some embarrassment later, because I told you when I was going up to Great Lakes to get a plaque or something, because I had spoken to the recruits and they had heard that I was in the first group. But they had a picture somewhat similar to that one there, made from the official Navy photograph, and I wasn't there. I had to get my congressman and everybody else, got the Time-Life organization to release the *Life* magazine picture to have it included in the Navy archives as the official photo of the group.* But the one that was really taken by the Navy photographer, I was not in.

Q: Did you have knowledge at that time that you'd been investigated by the FBI?**

---

*"First Negro Ensigns," *Life*, 24 April 1944, page 44.
**The backgrounds of prospective members of the first black officer candidate school were investigated thoroughly before the individuals were chosen for the training.

Justice White: Sure. I had worked in the Department of Justice before I went in. Sure.

Q: What was your reaction to that? Did it bother you?

Justice White: No. I expected it. And they do that for everybody. I thought they did it for everybody. I anticipated it and it happened. I think my father told me about the investigation.

Q: When I talked with you before, you mentioned prosecuting some of the cases of individuals who were making anti-American statements. And Arbor has subsequently told me that he was reading speeches on behalf of dissident groups. I'm surprised that didn't come out in an investigation.

Justice White: I am too. Arbor has a very vivid memory. He has a very vivid memory, and the longer things go on, the more vivid it becomes.

Q: You're suggesting he remembers things that didn't happen?

Justice White: Oh, I won't say that, although I must confess I have grown more forgetful too.

Q: What are your recollections of Jesse Arbor from that time in the training period?

Justice White: He was probably one of the guys that was loose as a goose, more loose than the rest of us. He would go on and hit the sack. He would say, "All this is a lot of bullshit. I'm hitting the sack."

Q: Did you find his humor a useful antidote to the program?

Justice White: Oh, sure. Sure. It relieved the pressure.

Q: Do you remember any specific types of humor that he would inject?

Justice White: I think there were jokes about previous assignments and future assignments in the Navy, saying somebody would probably be sent up there to the Aleutians.

Q: That was a joke that was still current when I was going through officer training 20 years later.
   What do you remember about Phillip Barnes?

Justice White: He loved the sea. He really loved the sea. His ambition was to become a fisherman. A quiet, gentle, big man--big, fat Barnes.

Q: I gather he was self-conscious about his appearance.

Justice White: He was fat. Is that what they said?

Q: Yes.

Justice White: He was a gentle, good man.

Q: Do you recall the basis for his love of the sea?

Justice White: No. Apparently he had some duty up in the Boston Harbor before he came back. I gather he had some duty up there, and he liked it. Indeed, his ambition was, when he got to be a civilian, to get a boat and become a fisherman. Out of all of them, I don't know how many of them had been at sea before they went to the training, but apparently he, as an enlisted man, had seen some duty up there. Is that what the record shows?

Q: I don't know on his case. Arbor had had some sea duty in that area, which he remembers very fondly.

White #2 - 74

What are your recollections of Samuel Barnes?

Justice White: Studious, quiet. What I remember most is that because of his gentility and his athletic capacity, Commander Armstrong used to like to play badminton with him. I've forgotten whether he let the commander win or not. [Laughter]

Q: I'm pretty sure he did.

Justice White: Yes. I don't think I can emphasize too much something that I felt and possibly the rest of the guys felt it too. The leader of the group was Reginald Goodwin, either by virtue of his own intellect--not that it was all that much greater than mine or the rest, but he did have it. And he was especially close to Armstrong.

Q: What do you remember of his personality?

Justice White: I spoke at his funeral. I said then that he played a difficult role. And I think I told you this before. And he was the unofficial courier. I believe that the white power structure would make known their desires to him, believing that he would or asking that he transmit those desires to us. And we did the same thing. And also questions of information: "What are they doing about this?" And it's a role that really I didn't appreciate too much while he was performing it.

Q: Why not?

Justice White: Well, it smacks of being an Uncle Tom.* And it's a difficult role.

Q: Was it a useful role, nonetheless?

Justice White: From the vantage point of 40 years, I can say so. And yet he did that in a way that he held our respect because he was smart, and his information and assistance were accurate. But in the final analysis, that's what he was doing.

Q: Was he perceived as a teacher's pet type by the rest of the group?

Justice White: No, it's deeper than that. It's more like being a company man when you're with a group of unions.

Q: Hair recalled an incident in which Goodwin broke up a

---
*The term "Uncle Tom" is used, according to the dictionary, to describe "a black who is overeager to win the approval of whites (as by obsequious behavior or uncritical acceptance of white values and goals)." It derives from a character--a pious and faithful slave--in Harriet Beecher Stowe's 1852 novel Uncle Tom's Cabin.

White #2 - 76

dice game or a card game, because he felt that might jeopardize the chances of the group. Was that a sort of role that he assumed for himself?

Justice White: Yes, he would do that. He would do that.

Q: Do you remember any other such instances in which he exerted leadership or discipline?

Justice White: No, I don't even remember that, but that is in character. That's a good example of it. He was very conscious of all the background from that. See, he went into the Navy early, as early as Mummy did. He had a chance to become very familiar with Commander Armstrong and, indeed, many of the ship's company's blacks, who were chosen for ship's company later, after Goodwin was, because Goodwin was in personnel.* And he was commissioned to work in personnel, just as I was commissioned to work in public information.

Q: Williams had also had a close relationship with Armstrong. I take it, though, that he didn't operate in the same fashion during your training. How would you differentiate Williams's role with Armstrong from that of

---

*The term "ship's company" does not here refer literally to those serving in a ship. Rather, it describes those who were on the staff of the Great Lakes Naval Training Station, as opposed to those who were being trained.

Goodwin?

Justice White: He wasn't on that same wavelength at all. Nobody would ever think that Mummy had access to Commander Armstrong, nor would he bring back any word from Commander Armstrong as to what the commander wanted.

Q: Was there any resentment of Goodwin and the things he was doing?

Justice White: I hesitate, because I don't know how much is just my reaction, and as you can tell, my reaction wasn't the same as that of the rest of the men all the time.

Q: And it's interesting to see the variations in reactions. In part, those are determined by attitudes and predispositions.

Justice White: Looking back over more than 40 years, I can tell you now I resented it some, but I never resented it so much that I would say, "Goody, I don't like what you're doing." Just down deep, I guess my resentment was part of not liking the position I was in, where having such a courier and such an emissary was necessary.

Q: Is it possible that some of that feeling is more retrospective than it was at the time?

Justice White: Possible, but, you see, I dealt with Goodwin longer than they did, because I stayed in public relations and he stayed in personnel. And in the Navy, just like in civilian life, there's an interplay of the roles of personnel and public relations. I'll give you something that you can understand. The people I had working under me in public relations had been put in ship's company by whom? Goodwin. So they were under my command, but they had ties of affection and gratitude to Goodwin. It's a function of personnel to bring entertainment to the base, although in public information I worked closely with band music and entertainment.

Although selected by Armstrong, I never fancied myself a darling or a favorite of Armstrong. That boils down to this. Lena Horne was coming to the camp.* Even though I was in public information, I knew nothing about it. My men didn't tell me, and I didn't know about it. And so the thing was over almost, and there was a beautiful picture in the press. I can see it now--Ensign Goodwin in his sharp, white uniform, Lena Horne on his arm, and they're striding into the auditorium, right down the center aisle, and

---

*Lena Horne (1917-   ) is a long-time black singer. She still appears in advertisements in the 1990s because she looks younger than her calendar years.

they're flanked on all sides with just seas of Navy men--
beautiful public relations. My photographer, Mose Preston,
whom I love dearly, took it. I asked him, "Why didn't you
tell me this was happening, Preston?"

"I thought you knew about it, sir."

So I can't tell whether some of what I say now might be
colored by some events that happened later, like the
incident I'm talking about. We were both commissioned
then. But I still think that he played a difficult role,
and he played it well. And he played it so well that there
wasn't this resentment that you talk about. If there was,
it was never overt.

Q: What do you remember about Dalton Baugh from that
period?*

Justice White: Sincere. I think he had gone to Hampton.

Q: Yes, he had.

Justice White: And been proud of his contact with the
commander there. Very anxious to do what was right. He
and Jesse Arbor had gone to the same college in Arkansas.
I remarked, "How in the hell out of the workings of things

---

*Dalton Louis Baugh was a member of the Golden Thirteen.
He died before he could be interviewed by the Naval
Institute's oral history program.

they only pick 16 of us, and two dudes from an inconspicuous school named Arkansas AM&N got in this group?" Jesse says now that Dalton Baugh resented that. I thought it remarkable that Mummy and I from the same neighborhood in Chicago got into it. It was just a small school and whatnot, but Baugh thought it was a reflection on the school. I guess it was, but it wasn't intended.

Q: It sounds as if he was a sensitive man.

Justice White: Yes, he was sensitive. He was sensitive, but in the service, what the hell, you've got to be kind of rough and ready. I'm sensitive, too, but I lived with these guys. But I don't want to overemphasize these things. You're asking for details, and they are colorful, and they help you understand the dynamics. But the overall thing it was--and Cooper doesn't exaggerate--it was one for all and all for one. We were hurt when the guys didn't make it. I never did enjoy my commission as much as I could have if Mummy had made it. We rejoiced when something happened good. One man in the group, John Reagan, lost a member of his crew through an accident, and we were all hurt.*

---
*John Walter Reagan is a member of the Golden Thirteen. His oral history, which discusses the loss of the crew member, is in the Naval Institute collection.

White #2 - 81

Q: Williams says now he's not bothered by the fact that he wasn't commissioned. How did he react at the time?

Justice White: Mummy's a stiff-upper-lip kind of guy. I would have been devastated. But out of the excursion he had been given his third stripe.* Gee, my rank went up so fast, I couldn't keep up. I was a boot; then I was a third class, then by God, before I turned around, they gave me two more. [Laughter] I couldn't keep up with my pay. I didn't know what it was supposed to be.

No, Mummy took it well. Mummy took it well, I think. At least by now he has constructed a scenario that he can live with. That's the reason that I'm anxious you talk with Dille about it.**

I wouldn't be surprised if that isn't the reason, but what I am surprised at is that Navy intelligence and the FBI didn't know all about that before they put him in the damn class. Since they reached into so many men to get such a few, they didn't have to pick Mummy.

Q: That is surprising. Looking at it, obviously as an

---
*While going through officer training, the candidates were first class petty officers, denoted by three chevrons on the rating badge.
**In an oral history interview, Williams indicated that he was told by Lieutenant (junior grade) Dille in 1944 that he would not be commissioned because an FBI investigation had turned up the fact that he had been a labor organizer for railroad station redcaps. In an interview subsequent to this one with Justice White, Dille did not recall giving such an explanation to Williams.

outsider, I'm intrigued by the range of different types of individuals who were included in the group, as if that was deliberate. Say, two from a college in Arkansas, some who had postgraduate work, some who had just a bachelor's degree, some who had completed some college, and Lear, apparently who had none.* That may have been deliberate, rather than, say, picking all graduates or all master's degrees or what have you.

Justice White: I hadn't thought of that. I had not thought of that. I think, on the whole, the Navy does a pretty good job of personnel, and it's all right for me to say that, because I became an officer. But I've had a chance to look around, and I think considering the fact-- let's see who went to sea. They didn't send any old men to sea. Who had shipboard experience? Hair, who was one of the younger ones.

Q: Sublett.**

Justice White: Sublett.

---

*Charles Byrd Lear was a member of the Golden Thirteen. He died shortly after World War II.
**Frank Ellis Sublett, Jr., is a member of the Golden Thirteen. His oral history is in the Naval Institute collection.

Q: Martin.*

Justice White: But they didn't send old guys like Nelson and Goodwin and White.

Q: They did not send as many to sea as wanted to go to sea.

Justice White: And they picked the ones that got that experience too. I wonder why they didn't put me in the JAG Corps?**

Q: That's curious. There was not a JAG Corps per se at the time. There were law specialists.

Justice White: I knew that. It's a wonder they didn't do that. For example, Commander Armstrong wasn't above doing this, using black officers as a source of information. Because all black recruits in general service came through Great Lakes at that time, and he was in charge of that training, he really considered himself the "admiral of the black Navy." That's the reason I say overall he was good for the entire process, I believe, because he wanted that to be important, so he pushed for it.

---

*Graham Edward Martin is a member of the Golden Thirteen. His oral history is in the Naval Institute collection.
**JAG--In the late 1960s, the Navy created the Judge Advocate General's Corps for its legal specialists.

I remember seeing him when he was leaving the service. I was in Washington then. He came by my desk. He was then a captain. I told you this?

Q: I don't believe so.

Justice White: Anyhow, I got along with him better than Nelson did, but that isn't saying much. I congratulated him on the fourth stripe, and he said, "Yes, too bad I couldn't have gotten it earlier during the war, because there's so much more I could have done if I'd had the power of the fourth stripe." He was absolutely sincere in that. He would have done more, as he saw it from his southern aristocratic background.

Q: One reason I can hypothesize for this range of experience--that if all had had, say, postgraduate education, then outsiders might say, "You have to handpick the Negroes you make officers of."

Justice White: Yes. I have no idea who did it and what were the criteria and how the hell they happened to get me. I have a hypothesis which I've probably shared with you, as to why they got me.

Q: You said you sent out a news release, in effect.

Justice White: Yes.

Q: On the whole, would you say the Navy made a good-faith effort in commissioning the first black officers?

Justice White: Oh, yes. Mind you, what they wanted was politics: somebody who would get the word and carry it through. They wanted guys like us who were sincere enough to work hard and yet not buck. And it isn't entirely admirable that we did so well, but they picked guys who wouldn't buckle under and get mad and fly off. We had only one of us who was more inclined to want to break out of the bounds, and that was Nelson, and he stayed in the Navy! I'll never figure that out. Here he hated Commander Armstrong the most. But he had guts.

Nobody's ever asked me about the evaluation of the Navy's implementation of Forrestal's policy of nondiscrimination, of affording greater opportunity for blacks and getting Lester Granger to go make that trip. Has anybody ever written anything about that?

Q: I'm not aware of it. It could have been.

Justice White: Let me just give you a thumbnail, and

that's how I caught up with these guys. I stayed at Great Lakes most all my tour there. If I had known everything was so history-making, I would have stolen and kept copies of the news releases. But we sent out more news releases relating to Great Lakes and the U.S. naval hospital, almost rivaling the lines of type got by the Army. We had to cater to home town stuff. We did that even before home town news came out, and took advantage of returning Navy people at the hospital and whatnot. We had an excellent photographer and a couple of good writers, and we had a CBS radio broadcast that came on on Sunday night.

I forgot where I was going.

Q: You were talking about Lester Granger.

Justice White: Well, a couple of things happened. There was Port Chicago, and the Navy decided, "Never again will we have a shore installation that's 100% black. We're going to scatter these guys throughout the service, because this just looks bad." And it did look bad, and it was bad. So they got no more than such and such a percent of any shore installation that would be black. But you had blacks all over the globe.

So Forrestal said to Lester Granger, who was the head of the National Urban League, "I want you to go find out how Navy policy is being implemented at these far places."

By that time I was in Washington, and they sent me along as a public information officer, to accompany Lester Granger on this tour. Now, of course, I had been in Washington, sleeping well and eating well. [Laughter] And we went in a fine plane that was ordinarily used by the Secretary of the Navy, and I visited these places. I met Dille in Hawaii.

Anyhow, I remember I picked up Arbor in Guam, Nelson in Eniwetok. We went all the way out to New Guinea. I don't think anybody got that far, at least not while I was there. Sublett, I think, was on Eniwetok.

Q: Yes, he was. Martin was also.

Justice White: I guess I should have felt a little bit of shame, you know, I was living so good when those poor devils weren't, but I didn't feel ashamed at all. In fact, it kind of tickled me a little bit.

Q: What was the substance of the trip? What were you doing?

Justice White: Well, the substance, I can sum it up. The purpose of the trip was to see whether the Navy, in its remote places, was taking advantage of the opportunity to utilize fully Negro personnel, or were they restricting

White #2 - 88

them, or restricting their use of them, to the more traditional roles. Lester Granger's findings, as I remember, were the farther you get from Washington, the less impact the words of the Secretary of the Navy had. Once again, you see how public relations and personnel kind of get mixed up. That's a trip that Goodwin, with his personnel expertise, could well have taken, but they did it the other way around.

Q: By "farther from Washington," you're saying that the less equal opportunity was implemented.

Justice White: Yes.

Q: Why do you say that it was not completely admirable that the group did so well?

Justice White: Well, maybe I'm talking about myself. Maybe I should have been more feisty. For instance, I remember a time when Commander Armstrong came in to me, and he said, "Did you hear what happened up at Hastings?"*

I'd heard two things happened up at Hastings. I heard, one, there had been an explosion there. I had also heard that there had been a near mutiny. I said, "Are you referring to the explosion, sir?"

_____
*Hastings, Nebraska, was the site of a supply depot.

White #2 - 89

"No, I'm referring to that ruckus up there." I had heard a little bit about the meeting up there, but I didn't become a naval officer to become a stool pigeon. What I heard was thirdhand, anyhow. If there had been some real insurrection there, I would have reported it. But the reaction was the sort I might expect. I think it was an ammunition depot, and they had a large number of blacks involved in handling ammunition; they got blown up. At least that's why they were complaining.

Q: I think this lack of feistiness that you talk about was couched in the atmosphere of the time, just as Branch Rickey recognized what was necessary to make his experiment succeed.

Justice White: I don't hang my head in shame, although I don't go around and boast about it--like that conversation I told you that I was subjected to when they were considering me for the commission.

Q: What was it about Nelson's personality that made him that way?

Justice White: I don't know. I don't know.

Q: What more do you remember about Nelson? What examples

White #2 - 90

are there of his personality?

Justice White: He had a beautiful blue road convertible, and he washed it every day. Oh, he loved guns. He'd put that .45 on, with his hat jauntily off to the side, not straight like the Navy tells you to wear it. Smart. I think that the group they picked had high IQs; I think Nelson's was. He took pride in his work. He kidded that he was put in charge of the remedial program for people who came to the Navy without enough education. And he referred to it as "Knucklehead University." He kidded it. It's an assignment that he might well have not liked. When I saw him on Eniwetok, he was proud of his shell collection. It was almost like being proud of his basket weaving. What else are you going to be proud of when you're on Eniwetok?

Q: It sounds as if the word "pride" was invented for Nelson.

Justice White: So it was an unusual group of people, and Cooper does not exaggerate when he said there was a strong feeling of camaraderie. However much they kept us in, it was enough to ensure that. And I do know, although it's not consistent with my going to see Claude Barnett of the Associated Negro Press, but perhaps it being wartime, I was asking him to keep it quiet, too, and if that were true, he would do it. But for some reason or another, here's something good the Navy was doing, and they didn't want anybody to know it. It struck me as silly then, sounds silly now.

Q: It suggests that there were at least some doubts at that point of whether you would succeed.

Justice White: If we were going to make it. I wondered. That's one of the things that we got word leaked to us, as to whose commission was in Washington, something had been signed or something, who was on the list.

Q: This came from Barnes's sister?

Justice White: Yes, I think so. That's the kind of information we got from her.

Q: What else do you remember about Cooper from that period?

Justice White: I don't know. He didn't have a role like Goodwin. He wasn't a clown like Arbor, and I mean that in the good sense. Cooper was serious. He had not been to sea like Phillip Barnes. I don't know where Cooper went. Where did he go?

Q: He went right back to Hampton.

Justice White: A rather staid person. He was cerebral, just like he is now. He's a thinker.

Q: He strikes me as a man of vision. Was he that way then?

Justice White: [Laughter] It's kind of hard to be a man of vision when you're in barracks number 202 in Camp Robert Smalls and there's a gate around. I guess you could be a man of vision. I don't know. If you had asked me then or now whether he was then a man of vision, I don't know whether he was or not. I don't remember his sharing his dreams with us, but I bet he wasn't in that card game that Goodwin said, "Don't do it." He wouldn't have been in it in the first place. Neither was I. He would be one of those like Goodwin who would say, "Break it up."

Q: What was it about him that would keep him apart from the card game?

Justice White: Just what you responded. And I guess in that sense he is a man of vision. He could see what hell would break loose if it would ever get out, you know. It's pride too. His wife just sent me a law review article written by their daughter, who's a graduate of Harvard Law School. It's in the field of evidence, among the subjects of the law that I count myself a minor league expert on.

Q: Well, I can see some vision beyond the barracks there that perhaps he, more than others, would feel this sense of representing a larger group, and maybe feeling some pressure therefore because of the opportunity it represented.

Justice White: I've always said that we were lucky. The Navy reached down into a group of over 100,000 men and picked up 13 of us as officers. They could have dipped this hand into that pool and come up with 13 more and 13 more and 13 more easily. And we were not unique.

Q: It could have picked 13 Nelsons, or it could have picked 13 Goodwins. It got a mixture.

Justice White: Yes. And I think they were lucky, and I would attribute it to luck, except for the fact that otherwise I think that the Navy had a pretty good Bureau of Personnel in those days. They did a pretty good job. For example, we complained about Armstrong. Who else could have been there during that transition? Here's a man who had ties to the antebellum South, who was a graduate of Annapolis. And they're about to bring in some blacks. They could have picked a do-gooder from the North. See, he could sell the program to the southern mentality of the Navy. "Don't tell me about the South. I'm from the South," Armstrong could say. "Don't tell me about Annapolis. I went there." And so, although Nelson hated it, I can see now that Armstrong was pretty good.

The thing I did not like about Armstrong from my little point of view was that he did have his pets, and I was not one of them. [Laughter] I guess it was that that I didn't like. How I got commissioned--maybe I disappointed him, I don't know. By then I guess I knew Armstrong.

Q: Disappointed him in what sense?

Justice White: I did my duty. I wasn't a fund of information. I didn't seek his counsel or company. Orders were given, and I obeyed them. Then I had the advantage, too. Back in those days we had naval districts. Are you old enough to remember naval districts?

Q: Yes, I was brought in through the Ninth Naval District.

Justice White: Well, I had dual assignments. Really, since public relations was a function of the district, I had detached duty to the naval training station, of which

Armstrong was a part. So really my line boss was the admiral of the naval district, of which I was very happy, because I wasn't thoroughly under the aegis of Armstrong.

Q: What do you recall of James Hair from that period, other than the "salty sock" remark?

Justice White: Hair didn't stick around much. He came in, we were together in officer training, and he left. I knew from his talk that he was from Florida. He was conscientious about working. Other than that, I really don't recall. I didn't know what happened to him after he left the officer training. I can't remember any anecdote that reveals. But you see him now, and that's what you see now--he was the same way then.

Q: He's very open, very enthusiastic.

Justice White: Yes, yes. And he thinks that all of this is very serious. You and I know it's not. [Laughter]

Q: Why not?

Justice White: I don't know.

Q: What do you remember about Charles Lear?

Justice White: He struck me as being strong, taciturn, the least talkative maybe out of all of us. He was a company commander before he was brought in. He was made a warrant officer, but he could lead men. He struck me as being strong and tough, not a guy who talks a lot.

Jesse and Lear were on Guam at the same time, I believe.

Q: Yes.

Justice White: When they told them both, maybe, "We don't allow officers down in such-and-such a quarters after dark," I don't know this, but I believe the anecdote is, Lear says, "I'm going down." He was that kind of guy. He was very conscious of his lack of education. I don't think he had any college.

Q: I don't think so, no.

Justice White: And that might have shown up a little bit in his grades, but he did so well in everything else. He struck me as being tough in the good sense of the word. If I wanted somebody who would not get jittery under fire, not at all, I'd pick Lear.

Q: Did he need more help than the rest with the curriculum?

Justice White: He might have. I don't know. Did some people say he did?

Q: I don't recall specifically. I just have heard that he had less education than the rest.

Justice White: I do kind of remember some tutoring in Navy regs. Yes, we did break down into groups for some of the study sessions. Cooper is accurate in that. I don't think it had quite the structure, at least in my mind, that he might have given the impression. But, now, in that connection, with us breaking down to help, did Lear receive any extra? I don't remember.

Q: What knowledge do you have of his sad demise?

Justice White: I saw him the day of the night he killed himself. I choose my words carefully, because I'd rather believe that than believe another story you may have heard of his death.* He and I were both living in Lake Forest. We didn't have much contact, but I saw him in downtown Lake Forest; that's a nice suburb of Chicago, not too far from Great Lakes. As a matter of fact, I moved there because I was at Great Lakes before I got shipped out.

---

*In Jesse Arbor's oral history, he contends that Lear was shot by his wife.

He had stayed in the Navy a bit longer than I had, and he had not yet got a job. And he was feeling not exactly sad, but he was uneasy about the fact he hadn't picked up a job yet. I assured him that a man of his talents could certainly get one, because he had what the world needs. I think he made some mention of perhaps going back in the Navy. We didn't discuss it in depth. I didn't think he looked so sad he was going to kill himself, no.

Q: Did he seem unhappy over the fact that he was no longer in the Navy?

Justice White: I think so. I think so.

Q: I have heard that suggested as perhaps a prime cause for his unhappiness.

Justice White: Could be. Could be. I won't say it wasn't, because as I remember, he was a farm boy from Iowa, and he probably never had a chance to command people. As he looked back at civilian life, he couldn't see himself having the kind of power he had in the Navy in civilian life, nor that kind of status either.

Q: In that he didn't appear a man on the verge of suicide, you must have been surprised when you got that news.

Justice White: Yes. Of course, you know, I've played back that conversation in my mind and asked myself, "Was there something that I could have said?" You know, kind of a fruitless effort. It's made me conscious of the fact, though, that people can be walking around with things on their minds and you not know it. I've tried to be more alert to unspoken feelings than I was then, although I haven't criticized myself too much for not saying anything.

Q: You can't read a mind.

Justice White: You've heard another version of that. That's so bizarre. I wouldn't believe it unless I got proof beyond a reasonable doubt.

Q: Jesse Arbor suggested it was homicide. Is that an example of his vivid memory?

Justice White: If it is, then I'm revealing my tendency not to be faced with what I don't want to be, unless it's right there where I can't avoid it.

Q: What do you recall of Graham Martin?

Justice White: Gentle. Here's a guy who was a vicious football player. Although he never was great big--I think he was a tackle.

Q: Yes, he was.

Justice White: He wasn't a big tackle, even for those days. Gentle, quiet, never the aggressor. Polite. Quiet, polite, not too outgoing.

Q: The type who would submerge resentments.

Justice White: Oh, yes. I mean--see, Great Lakes in those days, because it was true in the white world--no, let's get things straight. In athletics in even the Big Ten, the knighted Big Ten, blacks did not play basketball. That sounds ridiculous. Imagine, blacks played football but not basketball. Prejudice is not a logical thing. So why it was all right for them to play football? I guess because they had more clothes on. I don't know. But not basketball. And Great Lakes followed that same pattern. Great Lakes had a black basketball team, but they had one football team and one black player, and that was Graham Martin. I don't know. I remember him playing, but for his size and out there with his desire to make it, you can imagine he took a lot of punishment.

I do remember when Buddy Young was playing for

Illinois, and Illinois came up and played Great Lakes.* And they had those recruits there. Buddy Young would score a touchdown against Great Lakes, the recruits stood up and said, "Yea!"--much to the embarrassment of the brass that here our recruits are yelling for Illinois, rather than yelling for the Navy.

That was my recollection of Graham Martin, a very quiet man, not too outgoing, but very nice.

Q: What do you remember from John Reagan from your time together?

Justice White: Looked like half the guys in this thing had played football. I mentioned Graham Martin. I think both Baugh and Arbor had played some football.

Q: Yes, and Sublett and Sam Barnes.

Justice White: Sam had played football?

Q: Yes.

Justice White: I didn't know that. I don't think I knew

---

*Claude H. "Buddy" Young was a 5-4, 175-pound halfback who played for the University of Illinois in 1944 and 1946 with a year in between for naval service. He later played professional football for the New York Yankees, 1947-51; Dallas Texans, 1952; and Baltimore Colts, 1953-55. Young was elected to the College Football Hall of Fame in 1968.

it then. I knew that he was an athlete, that physical ed was his field, but I didn't know he played football. I guess I was more aware of Reagan's football, because he played at Montana. I regarded that as being more big league than the other football these other guys had played. I don't know what football Graham Martin had played before he played for the Navy. I don't know if he won a Big Ten letter.

Q: Yes, he was at Indiana.

Justice White: Had he won his letter at Indiana?

Q: I don't know whether he had a letter, but he said he was as good as the people who were playing more often.

Justice White: Reagan had come from Chicago. I did not know him. He was much younger than I was. But I related more to his football experience because I think he had gone to Lindbloom, and that was a school that used to trounce the school I went to. I guess I didn't know much about the background of Reagan. I haven't read your story.

You were asking me what kind of guy he was. Looks like I'm using some of the same words. Cooper fancies himself an intellectual, and he is. Nelson was older, and he thought he was pretty smart. He had worked for the

Urban League, and he knew his way around. Goodwin also had been a YMCA worker and had been around and had been in the adult world, so he figured he was pretty smart.* Reagan was so young, he had not been much in the adult world, except as a football player. I don't know if he had ever been a clerk or social worker or something like that. But he was never diffident because of that. He was always confident of his capacity to think. I would describe him as most of the time satisfied with just being right himself, without trying to convince somebody else of it.

Q: Sublett was the same age as Martin. What do you remember of him? In fact, they were born the same day.

Justice White: That is right. How old are they?

Q: They were born in 1920.

Justice White: I was born in '14. Sublett was not as rollicking as Jesse Arbor. Nobody was. Sublett was nice and loose, somewhat loose, and of the younger group. He had not had life experiences or Navy experiences, I think, that commanded a lot of attention from us. Let's put it this way--from what he did in the Navy and his attitude towards things, I wasn't surprised when he came out and was

---
*YMCA--Young Men's Christian Association.

in charge of the repair department of a new-car agency. He was a motor mach, I think, before he became an officer.

Q: Yes.

Justice White: I would expect him to do that. I would have been very much surprised if he had been just a mechanic there. He was on the level of being supervisor of that department. I wasn't surprised when he became a model either.

Q: Is there any conclusion you would draw from the fact that so many in the group were football players?

Justice White: Yes. Don't forget these blacks were picked by whites. Whites said, "Gee whiz, if I'm going to get somebody to lead other blacks, maybe I'd better get a big one."

Q: All the football players weren't big, though.

Justice White: They were bigger than Cooper and White and Nelson. And don't forget, for their day I guess they must have been big in size. Sublett, Arbor, Reagan, Baugh were all over six feet. Don't forget in our day that was tall.

Q: John Bulkeley, the PT boat hero who took MacArthur out of the Philippines, was specifically looking for football players among white officer candidates for aggressive-type assignments.* That may have been a factor also.

Justice White: I do think, though, those that engaged in team sports learned something about sticking together for a single role. Maybe that says something. See, I ran track. I was on my own. Me first, to heck with you other guys.

Q: Williams was also a track man.

Justice White: Yes, yes, yes, but he wasn't as fast as I was.

Q: Well, it's an irony that having picked the men with the football background, that they were not used to potential after commissioning.

Justice White: Some of them were already too old. Arbor and Baugh were too old. Sublett wasn't, but I don't think they were playing at it. Reagan's the only guy who played after the Navy.

Q: No, but I mean they didn't get into combat assignments

---

*Lieutenant Commander John D. Bulkeley, USN; General Douglas MacArthur, USA.

that might have taken advantage of those characteristics.

Justice White: I see. Well, they didn't have a body of men whom they could send them to. You see, after we were commissioned, they still were trying to put together an all-black boat or ship. Let's see—Hair got aboard one.

Q: He was in the Mason.

Justice White: Yes, and then the PC-1264 had Gravely.*

Justice White: Did any of us get on there?

Q: I don't think so.

Justice White: Let's see. Gravely came out of Hampton, too, didn't he?

Q: Right.

Justice White: There again, just look at Gravely. I think the Navy picked the right one to be an admiral. Jesus, shaking his hand is like shaking an oak tree. The Navy

---

*For a detailed history of this ship, see Eric Purdon, Black Company: The Story of Subchaser 1264 (Washington-New York: Robert B. Luce, Inc., 1972).

White #2 - 107

does a good job of that.

Q: What qualities did John Dille bring to the group that he's now included in the "thirteen plus one?"

Justice White: You know, John Dille and I were classmates in college.

Q: I think you mentioned that before.

Justice White: I didn't know it then. It wouldn't have made much difference. One, he was Armstrong's principal assistant, so much of the Armstrong communication and policy came through Dille. But I think Dille always exhibited a compassion and an understanding of how the black guys felt. Then, too, he was closer to them in age. Armstrong was older, and Armstrong had more rank, too, so that there was no communication with him. You just take the orders, except when you were playing badminton with him, like Sam Barnes.

I don't remember Dille being one of our instructors. It seems to me he was kind of like our chaperone or dean of the school of instructors, rather than one of the people that actually taught in class. Because Dille didn't know enough signaling or navigation or the usual things, Navy regs, to have taught it, because I guess he'd just gone through ensign school himself.

Q: Right.

Justice White: So I guess a visible interest and humanity that he exhibited.

Q: Did he provide useful moral support?

Justice White: Yes, yes. I don't even know why I hesitate so long on that, but I'm trying to see a scene where he drops in the barracks and we all hang around and he's saying something. I don't recall that, but if somebody can recall that, I certainly wouldn't say it's not true. I just feel it's the kind of thing that he did. I'm anxious to know what the other guys say about him. I should have read those papers.

Q: The memories vary widely. Cooper feels very warm toward him. Some of the others he didn't register that strongly with.

Q: Let me say this--but for Cooper and a few other persons, there would be no Golden Thirteen. We would have let the thing just sink below the surface without a ripple. And thank God for them. But that's a question that should

White #2 - 109

have been asked of Mummy. Mummy and Dille worked in ship's company for years together, and then whatever Dille did with the officers, Mummy would remember better than I do. Goodwin and Dille were close. Armstrong, Goodwin, Dille, and Mummy ran the black Navy for a while. But Dille somehow escaped being tarnished by the things that hurt Armstrong.

Q: What do you mean, things that hurt Armstrong?

Justice White: Well, the Navy's separatist policy was bad. Even though the people were in it, they didn't like it. Armstrong was the administrator of that policy. And although Dille was his lieutenant, he was not tarnished by that.

Q: It could be that he had a different attitude. He may have been what you call a northern do-gooder.

Justice White: I'm not saying he should have been tarnished by it; I'm just saying he was not tarnished by it. And I never felt like tarnishing him with it myself. There was something about his attitude and the way he did things that made you think that he was all right.

White #2 - 110

Q: Do you remember an officer named Van Ness?*

Justice White: Yes.

Q: What do you recall about him?

Justice White: I didn't have too much contact with him, but he was tarnished by it. Kauffold was not.** I've run across Kauffold. I don't know whatever happened to Van Ness, but I've run across Kauffold in civilian life. I was Director of Registration and Education for the state, and he was principal, I think, of a downstate school, Vance Kauffold. That's interesting. I don't really know why some get tarnished and some don't, but Kauffold was fake. He was supposed to be a good guy, but he was also under Armstrong, carrying out Armstrong's policies.

Q: Van Ness was an academy man who had not stayed on active duty, I think for physical reasons. He was sent there on orders, and he told me that afterward he expressed a desire not to be assigned to work with blacks again.

Justice White: He must have had some unpleasant experience.

---
*Lieutenant Commander Donald O. Van Ness, USNR. Van Ness has been interviewed about his experiences at Great Lakes as part of the Naval Institute's oral history program.
**Lieutenant Vance A. Kauffold, USNR.

Q: I think it was more a matter of attitude than unpleasant experiences.

What do you remember of the sequence of events when you did get your commission?

Justice White: When mine finally came through?

Q: Yes.

Justice White: The rest of the guys in the barracks were walking around with pants with a crease down the top, wearing hats and looking like officers. I felt awful for a while.

Q: Why the delay?

Justice White: I don't know. My serial number is lower than some of those guys. I don't know why. But maybe it wasn't all that long, but it seemed to me like it was a couple of months. But maybe it was just two or three days.

Q: It couldn't have been a couple of months. [Laughter]

Justice White: Seemed to be longer than that, though. No.

White #2 - 112

We were commissioned, and I think orders right then gave us our new duty stations. They began peeling off. The question was, "Where are you going? Where are you going?"

I said, "I'm staying."

Q: Do you remember taking an oath of office as an ensign?

Justice White: No. Did they give us the ceremonial oath of office?

Q: No one else remembers it. It's a standard thing for officers, though.

Justice White: I went to Washington. Then I became more conscious of the fact that I was a lawyer and wasn't a newsman. Up until then I had an office here at Great Lakes with a couple of guys that were pretty good newsmen. As I say, we turned out a lot of copy which gave a lot of good press to the Navy, and really doing this out of very little raw material.

Then they sent me down to Washington, and they put me in the press section of the public information office, where I had a desk with other lieutenants. I had no staff. I was staff then to the commanding officer, and we were doing stories. I recall the officer in charge--I forget his name now--he said, "White, you pick up the phone too.

Don't you wait for something black to turn up." So I thought that that was the ultimate of the integration, because I've told you before how when our radio show went on, "This is brought to you by the men of the Negro regiments of Great Lakes and men of the Negro companies of Great Lakes." It came down to finally there was no radio show at all, so you didn't need a person to look out after the Negro things at Great Lakes.

That's when I went down to Washington. There I handled regular press duty just like the other officers. Admittedly, when there was something with a racial angle to it, they would call upon me to give such expertise as I had. I enjoyed my stay down there.

Q: Why do you say that you were more conscious of yourself as a lawyer during that period?

Justice White: It's because I had to do the writing of the stories myself and not direct that they be done. Newsmen can sit at a typewriter and think into a typewriter, and I can't think into a typewriter. I've got that word processor there, and I can't think better with that. I have to get out the old pencil. There's a newsman here in town who was in the press section with me, and we talk about old times, talk about the time when a hush fell over the press section when I walked in.

Q: Were you the center of attention where you went, wearing an officer's uniform?

Justice White: Everywhere. Oh, God, a naval officer's uniform? Sure! You won't believe it now, but my head wasn't always bald, and I even had girls whistle at me. It was a heady experience.

Q: What sorts of living accommodations did you have to make in Washington?

Justice White: Not bad. It was a building not far from Howard University on Elm Street, Northwest, where I had a room. It was similar to living in a YMCA. I had a room and, I think, a shower right there in my room and everything. It was not bad.

Q: Did you give any thought at all to staying in the Navy after the war was over?

Justice White: Yes! Sure. Once. The commander who was in charge of the press section sent me a nice letter upon my leaving. He said, "Judge Hastie is being considered by the Senate for appointment as governor of the Virgin Islands. He will be entitled to have on his staff a naval

White #2 - 115

aide, and that position carries with it the rank of lieutenant commander."* At that time I was a jaygee. He said, "Why don't you go see him? Maybe you'll get a chance to make the step and become his naval aide." Judge Hastie later became judge of the Second Circuit Court of Appeals, but at that time he had been a district court federal judge and was being considered for this spot.

I went to see him. He said, "Number one, I'm just being considered by the Senate, and I make it a point I don't count something before it hatches. But then if they do approve of my appointment and if I do have a naval aide, the one thing I don't need is another lawyer. So I wouldn't be interested in appointing you to the task."

"Thank you very much, Judge." So my thought of shipping over ended with that conversation. At that time I could get another half-stripe if you shipped over. I had my job as assistant U.S. attorney waiting for me.

Q: In 1949, John Reagan got a letter inviting him to come back on active duty, which he did. Sublett got one, which he didn't follow up on. Were you ever invited back after that?

Justice White: I don't think so. See, I'd had no

---
*William H. Hastie (1904-1976) was the first black federal judge, appointed in 1937. He was governor of the Virgin Islands from 1946 to 1949, when he was appointed Judge of the U.S. Circuit Court of Appeals.

experience. Nelson once sent something out to us, I think, saying that they wanted some of us to come back.

Q: What are the highlights of your post-Navy career?

Justice White: Almost being appointed to the Supreme Court of Illinois, but not quite getting it.

Q: Why didn't you get it?

Justice White: Somebody else did, a Greek by the name of Justice Stamos, a very excellent judge, who was one of my colleagues in the court, and he got the nod.* This is the year of the Greeks.** Next year Jesse Jackson and me.***

No, I guess my life has not had any dramatic upturns. It seems to me that my life has been one gradual upward course. After third grade, I went into the fourth grade. After being a lawyer a number of years, I was appointed by Kerner, who had been my boss when he was United States

---
*Justice John T. Stamos was appointed to the Illinois Supreme Court in 1988.
**This interview was held during the 1988 Democratic National Convention that nominated Governor Michael Dukakis, a man of Greek ancestry, to run for President.
***Jesse Jackson, a black clergyman, contended for the Democratic Party's presidential nomination in 1988 before being beaten by Dukakis in a series of primaries.

White #2 - 117

attorney.* When he became governor, he asked me to join him in the cabinet, in a post I really enjoyed.

Q: What was that?

Justice White: I was Director of the Department of Registration and Education, and in that I was the licensing officer of the state. I also directed the state's research in the fields of water and oil and natural history. I was also chairman of the board of the state museum. I did all that for $15,000. Anyhow, I enjoyed it very much. Then I was elevated to the bench in 1964, and then in 1980, I was elevated to the Appellate Court, where I sit now as a presiding judge of the Third Division of the Appellate Court.

Q: Are there any specific incidents that stand out in your mind from this long judicial career?

Justice White: Yes. I was the judge who was author of the historical opinion that settled legally and judicially the fact that Washington forces were in control of the city

---

*Otto Kerner, Jr. (1908-1976) was governor of Illinois, 1961-68. He headed the President's National Advisory Commission on Civil Disorders which issued a report in 1968 warning that the United States was becoming racially divided into two "separate but unequal" societies.

council.* Washington was this city's first black mayor and had established a very sound principle that majority rules.** Isn't that profound? I took about 20 pages to say it, but it boiled down to that.

I don't know. You know, I've been in this business a long time. Which is the most? I was reading some of my opinions the other day--frankly, in connection with my aspirations for the Illinois Supreme Court. And I enjoyed reading some of them, and I thought some of them were significant. But of historic significance that will be cited 100 years from now by lawyers, like Marbury v. Madison? No.***

Q: What do you remember of your work with the Juvenile Court?

Justice White: I was amazed at the number of people who are conscientiously interested in trying to do something for kids, when so often nobody else cares. I think that's overall. And not all of the time the people trying to do something are on the right track, but, by golly, they're really trying--the fact that they're even trying when

---

*The legal citation for the ruling is Roti v. Washington (1986), 148 Ill. App. 3d 1006; 500 N.E.2d 463.
**Harold Washington, the first black mayor of Chicago, held that office from 1983 until his death in 1987.
***In 1803, in the case of Marbury v. Madison, the U.S. Supreme Court for the first time overturned a law passed by Congress.

nobody else cares. You can't imagine how alone and without anything for support.

I was not in the courtroom when a mother standing in court said that she did not want to take her child back home. Now there'd been a history in which the mother had said, "For my sanity and for the sanity and the safety of the other five kids at home, I can't take her back." And the girl wheeled around and jumped out of a plate glass window.

Q: You told me before that your appointment to the U.S. attorney's office was tokenism. At what point did you come to a conscious realization that the society was beyond tokenism? Or have you reached such a point?

Justice White: I don't know of any other institution in America where the institution is seeking blacks to play a leadership role. That's beyond tokenism.

Q: What importance would you ascribe to the naval experience in your whole life experience?

Justice White: I won't make that comparison, but let me say I guess I got a better appreciation for ordinary guys that could be drafted into the Army or Navy--not great, but an appreciation for their courage and capacity to think. I told you about that night when the men were not going to shove off, didn't I, up at Great Lakes?

Q: I don't remember it.

Justice White: I was on duty in some capacity as an officer, and since I was just on extra duty with the center and was really a district officer, my contact with center personnel was kind of tenuous, but we were all there in the same location together. On this night the word came to me that company so-and-so, an outgoing unit, was not going to shove off when they got orders to shove off. I didn't tell you that?

Q: I don't remember it, no.

Justice White: Again, from a public relations point of view, I knew hell was going to break loose here. So I went over to the barracks. I had no authority to be there. I guess I went with the petty officer who told me about this. Everything in the barracks was quiet and orderly, so quiet and orderly I was suspicious.

So I asked to speak to the petty officers there, and they said they had been introduced to this officer who was going to take them overseas as a logistic support company. And this guy, in introducing himself to the company, was

White #2 - 121

acquainting the company with some of his philosophy--something to the effect that the only good nigger was an obedient nigger, and they ought to know that. If those weren't his words, "nigger" was in them or something equally derogatory--and letting them know how tough he was and how he wasn't going to take any crap.

Oh, Jesus. So I asked the guys, "Cool it. Right now, if we let things stand as they are, the fault's entirely on him. If you guys disobey the orders, they'll forget why you're doing it, and the fault will be on you, and they'll never get to what is the real cause of it. So please, cool it. Let me get this information into the right hands."

I don't know how I did it now. I wish I could give you details of the person I went to to report that this had happened. But I sought out somebody that night, and I may not have been the only person to report this incident to the appropriate officer. What happened? They changed officers. The officer who said these remarks did not go with that company. I've long wondered--did he do that on purpose. Maybe he didn't want to go to Manus. Maybe he didn't want to go to New Guinea. One way of getting out of it is to do that. At any rate, whether that was his purpose or not, and whatever happened to him, I don't know, but that officer did not go with that company.

Q: I take it the company did go.

Justice White: Oh, they went.

Q: I asked the other men about the values they got from their parents that carried them into the naval experience and through life.

Justice White: You were asking what did the Navy give me. The thing I'm trying to illustrate--these weren't a bunch of Ph.D.'s that I was talking to. They were guys who had feelings and who could reason--and they had discipline. They had some petty officers that really had their men under control. They weren't being disorderly. They had made up their minds. They were not going to be disorderly. If they said, "Shove off," they weren't going to start.

Now, values from parents? Of course? What do you want--mother and apple pie and that kind of thing? You don't want that kind of thing.

Q: Well, you told me the business about the value of learning, and that's a thing that the whites can't take away from you. Were there teachings from your parents in the racial area?

Justice White: Sure. "If they call you nigger, you call them white trash." It never seemed to be quite adequate.

[Laughter] I don't know.

Q: Did they instill a pride in blackness?

Justice White: Sure. They were lifetime members of the NAACP and that kind of thing, although they didn't go around talking about it so much, as became fashionable later.* I lived in a peculiar neighborhood where the blacks were middle class and probably had more education than the white inhabitants of the area, about as much money. That was the time when a white streetcar conductor would probably make about the same amount of money as a black postal worker. I told my mother once, because I had seen drunken white men coming from a certain speakeasy that was in the neighborhood, I said, "You know what, Mama? I never saw a black man drunk."

She said, "Well, I've seen lots of them." So she was preparing me: "Don't think that whites get drunk and blacks don't." But that was the kind of social situation in which I grew up. But values?

Q: What did they teach you about tolerance and understanding?

Justice White: I don't think they taught me anything about
_____
*NAACP--National Association for the Advancement of Colored People.

that, because they lived it. My mother was a public school teacher; her children were 100% white. So she would come back home and talk to me about them. I don't know how to answer that. During the race riots, did my father buy a 30-30 rifle? You bet your boots he did. That's one of my earliest recollections. I think they happened about 1919.

Q: What part did religion play in the life of the family?

Justice White: Much. I went to Sunday school and church. My mother changed churches, and I changed Sunday school. I taught Sunday school. And I'm still searching. I gave an invocation in the last couple of weeks, and I said, "You're really taking an awful chance in asking me to give the invocation. I have been a Congregationalist, a Christian Scientist, and I'm now Roman Catholic. I have one daughter who is a dues-paying member of a Jewish reform temple, another daughter who's a follower of Buddha. If you think with that background I'm going to ad lib my prayer, you're mistaken. I'm going to stick to the thing that's written there." So I have a mixed-up religious background.

Q: Are those the only two children you have, two daughters?

White #2 - 125

Justice White: Yes.

Q: Those are the twins then.

Justice White: Yes.

Q: What sort of work are they in now?

Justice White: Carolyn has a radio talk show on an ABC radio affiliate in San Francisco. Marilyn is a nurse-midwife. Her husband is a family medicine specialist, so she births them and he takes care of them, but they don't work together.

Q: I guess, finally, I have an interest in your observations on the role of the Golden Thirteen today, those of you who are left.

Justice White: At times I thought we were about as relevant as World War II ships, but I think at this last meeting I became convinced, when you break things down for me so I can digest it. I don't know that I want to be pointed out as a walking relic, like you go visit something, an old gray-haired man and whatnot. But they've convinced me that we can be helpful in recruiting, and some of our guys are doing a good job. And I do believe in the

Navy as an institution.

I am going to be more active during this coming year in their officer recruitment program. There's a black man, a black officer--I forget his name; I forget names. He said, "Each of you guys get us one." I like that. Quantifiable. Not go around and making speeches. If I can point to this guy, I marched him all through the process and he's in, signed. I'm going to have that as my goal. I hope I can get two, but I like that aspect of it. No, I'm not the believer that this is all great, like some of my colleagues. And I'm glad they feel that way, because if everybody had been like me, then there wouldn't have been a Golden Thirteen.

I do think that I'm one of those who came up with the idea that, "Since we can't get a ship named after us, why not a building?" But it is not surprising that some other people came up with the idea, too, but I know that I advanced it. I think it's more appropriate, too, because most of us were not on ships, and this will reach a whole lot more people than a ship would.

Q: What are your recollections of the ceremony last year when that was dedicated?

Justice White: Wonderful! And I was all set to get mad. That little gal, Admiral Hazard, Bobby Hazard, a stubborn person.* I'd run across her in conferences, and I hit her with everything I could. I said, "Dear, you won't delay this from June to July? Coincidentally, the NNOA will be here in July." I could see the public relations: "These our progeny and this is the beginning." She wouldn't do it. I said, "We waited 40 years for this, and you won't wait one month." She wouldn't do it. And she kept giving me cockamamy answers that I did not accept, but she stuck to her guns.

Q: What was her reason?

Justice White: A very human one, and she won me completely, not only by her graciousness and not only by the fact that she wore her uniform well, but also she said, "I, too, am a pioneer. And I want to be part of the celebration, where we're celebrating your pioneering efforts." I don't know why she didn't tell me that in the first place.

Q: She was due to leave, was that it?

Justice White: Yes! And she'd get a new duty station, and she wanted to be part of it. Bless her heart, she did a jam-up job. I was all set to be real angry. I still think

---
*Rear Admiral Roberta L. Hazard, USN, Commander Great Lakes Naval Training Center, July 1985-July 1987.

White #2 - 128

it would have been a bigger thing, but I got her point of view, and I applaud her for it. Do you know where she is now?

Q: No, I don't.*

Justice White: What did some of the other guys say?

Q: Well, they certainly enjoyed it. It's sort of a capstone to the experience, a recognition, albeit very late, of what you achieved.

Justice White: Yes, yes.

Q: It's ironic that the group has become so much more revered and paid attention to in retrospect than at the time.

Justice White: Well, I don't know. Revered, yes, but we were reviled then. There were articles in the paper, Life magazine. People intelligent enough to read Life magazine decrying the fact that the Navy was lowering its standards to admitting blacks to the officer ranks.

---

*In August 1987, Rear Admiral Hazard reported for duty as Director, J-1 (Manpower and Personnel), Joint Chiefs of Staff.

Q: I read the letters to the editor that were in Life a few weeks after your photo appeared.*

Justice White: That's where it was. But it was a good trip. It was a good trip. I think we did some good. Well, no, I know we did some good. I know we did some good. These guys are so good that there are some bad things I don't even contemplate as being possible. We knew nobody of our group was going to go out on a weekend and come back drunk. We knew nobody was going to be caught doing something dishonest or vicious or really indiscreet. We took that as a given. I got to thinking that that doesn't necessarily follow when you get a bunch of young guys together. It could go the other way. But we were so sure of that quality that it didn't even cross my mind, and I have a suspicious mind.

Q: Branch Rickey picked Jackie Robinson very carefully. I would say that the Navy picked your group very carefully.

Justice White: They were lucky.

---

*The 15 May 1944 issue of Life published a series of letters in response to the photo of the black ensigns and an editorial titled "Negro Rights." The pro and con responses in the letters represented some of the prevailing attitudes on race relations of the period.

White #2 - 130

Q: That's your view, obviously. [Laughter]

Justice White: Yes. [Laughter] But I think the result was good. I've already boasted about--too bad I can't document it. But I did my job well. I'm sorry that at this late date, in the black community, the Navy is still behind the eight ball. I don't quite get why. I don't know what they're going to have to do so that when people ask for service of preference, they'll pick anything but the Navy. So I'm going to try to be a salesman for it.

Q: Great. Thank you again very much for your contribution to the record.

Justice White: For what it's worth.

Index to
Reminiscences of
Justice William Sylvester White

Alves, A.
    Enlisted Navy man who went through officer training with the Golden Thirteen in early 1944 but was not commissioned, 68-69

Arbor, Jesse W.
    Golden Thirteen member who had experience as a quartermaster before undergoing officer training at Great Lakes, Illinois, in early 1944, 38, 60; assessment of, 71-72

Armstrong, Captain Daniel W., USNR (USNA, 1915)
    As officer-in-charge of Camp Robert Smalls, oversaw the training of black officers and enlisted men at Great Lakes, Illinois, during World War II, 45, 52, 74, 76, 78, 88-89, 106, 109-110; aristocratic in manner but sincerely interested in advancing the status of black naval personnel, 56-57, 83-85, 93-95

Army, U.S.
    Fort Sheridan, north of Chicago, was involved in a lawsuit concerning hand grenades in the early 1940s, 12; the Army was the preferred service for black enlistees during World War II, far ahead of the Navy, 33; pushed for unification of U.S. armed services at the end of World War II, 41

Athletics
    Black sailors were permitted only limited participation on the sports teams at the Great Lakes Naval Training Station during World War II, 22, 100; several of the members of the Golden Thirteen were excellent athletes, 99-101, 104-105

Barnes, Phillip G.
    Golden Thirteen member whose sister fed information to the black officer candidates at Great Lakes, Illinois, in early 1944, 36-37, 54-55, 91; assessment of, 73

Barnes, Samuel E.
    Golden Thirteen member who was quiet and studious while undergoing officer training at Great Lakes, Illinois, in early 1944, 74, 101-102

Barnett, Claude
    As head of the Associated Negro Press, talked with White during World War II about the training of black Navy men, 55-56, 90-91

Baugh, Dalton L.
    Golden Thirteen member who had gone to a small segregated college in Arkansas before undergoing officer training at Great Lakes, Illinois, in early 1944, 79-80

Black Naval Officers
    See Golden Thirteen; National Naval Officers Association

Camp Robert Smalls
    Location of recruit training for White at Great Lakes, Illinois, in late 1943, 18-25; location of officer training for the first black officers in early 1944, 28-31, 36-37, 45-47, 51, 57-69; public relations for the black sailors in the camp in 1944-45, 31-33; black singer Lena Horne provided entertainment for Navy men at the camp during World War II, 78-79

Chicago, Illinois
    Site of White's education and upbringing in the 1920s and 1930s, 1-7; White began his practice of law in Chicago in the late 1930s, 7-10; White worked as an assistant U.S. attorney in Chicago from 1939 to 1943, 10-15

Cooper, George C.
    Golden Thirteen member whose back was injured during officer training at Great Lakes, Illinois, in early 1944, 67; a serious, cerebral person, 91-93; helped bring the group back together in recent years, 108

Depression
    Economic conditions in the 1930s forced White's parents to make sacrifices so he could go to college and law school, 2-3; White found it difficult to get a job as a lawyer in 1937 because the Depression was still in effect, 7-8

Destroyer Escorts
    The USS Mason (DE-529) was commissioned in World War II with a crew of black enlisted men, 36, 38-40

Destroyers
    The Navy got excellent publicity from a Golden Thirteen reunion on board the USS Kidd (DDG-993) in 1982, 48

Dickerson, Earl B.
    Noted Chicago lawyer for whom White worked in the late 1930s, 5-6, 8, 10

Dille, Lieutenant (junior grade) John F., Jr., USNR
    Served as a battalion commander for training of black sailors at Great Lakes, Illinois, in 1944 and provided moral support for members of the Golden Thirteen, 28-29, 107-109

Education
   White's education in Chicago public schools in the 1920s and at the University of Chicago in the 1930s, 1-2, 7; White's parents stressed to him the value of education, 6; literacy training for black recruits at Great Lakes, Illinois, in 1944, 45, 90

Eniwetok Atoll
   Site of a Pacific Navy base that employed black naval personnel during World War II, 45, 87, 90

FBI
   See Federal Bureau of Investigation

Federal Bureau of Investigation
   Did not have black agents in the early 1940s, 16; conducted an investigation in 1943 of the black enlisted men who were being considered for officer training, 70-71, 81

Forrestal, James V.
   Secretary of the Navy who sent former National Urban League official Lester Granger on a tour of Navy facilities near the end of World War II to see how well the service's policy on integration was being implemented, 42-43, 85-88

Fort Sheridan, Illinois
   Army post north of Chicago that was involved in a lawsuit concerning hand grenades in the early 1940s, 12

Golden Thirteen
   Black enlisted men who received officer training in segregated Camp Robert Smalls at Great Lakes, Illinois, in early 1944, 28-31, 36-37, 45-47, 51, 57-69; assessments of individual members of the group, 36, 45-47, 71-85, 89-104; the Navy got excellent publicity from a Golden Thirteen reunion on board the destroyer Kidd (DDG-993) in 1982, 48; Life magazine published a photo of the group in an April 1944 issue, 70; the assignments given to the group following their commissioning generally did not take advantage of their qualifications, 105-106; role of the group in Navy recruiting in the 1980s, 125-126; in 1987 the Great Lakes Naval Training Center dedicated an in-processing building to honor the group, 126-128; assessment of the group's achievements, 129-130

Goodwin, Reginald E.
   Golden Thirteen member who served in leadership and communication roles for the black enlisted men who were undergoing officer training at Great Lakes, Illinois, in early 1944, 45-47, 74-79, 103

Granger, Lester B.
　Former National Urban League official who made a trip to Navy facilities near the end of World War II to see how well the service's policy on integration was being implemented, 42-43, 85-88

Gravely, Vice Admiral Samuel L., Jr., USN (Ret.)
　As the Navy's first black three-star admiral, he achieved a status not accorded blacks in private industry, 49-50; assessment of, 106-107

Great Lakes (Illinois) Naval Training Center
　Dedicated in 1987 an in-processing building to honor the Golden Thirteen, 126-128

Great Lakes (Illinois) Naval Training Station
　Location of recruit training for White in late 1943, 18-25; location of officer training for the first black officers in early 1944, 28-31, 36-37, 45-47, 51, 57-69; White remained at Great Lakes as a public information officer following his commissioning in March 1944, 31-35, 86, 112; literacy training for black recruits at Great Lakes in 1944, 45, 90; black singer Lena Horne provided entertainment for Navy men at Camp Robert Smalls during World War II, 78-79; White calmed black naval personnel who didn't want to obey an order because of the prejudiced attitude of the officer who gave it during World War II, 120-122

Hair, James E.
　Golden Thirteen member who served in the USS Mason (DE-529) in 1945, following commissioning as an officer in 1944, 36, 39; was reunited with other members of the Golden Thirteen on board the USS Kidd (DDG-993) in 1982, 48; assessment of, 95

Hastie, William H.
　Federal judge who served as governor of the Virgin Islands from 1946 to 1949, 114-115

Hazard, Rear Admiral Roberta L., USN
　As Commander Great Lakes Naval Training Center, presided at the 1987 dedication of an in-processing center to honor the Golden Thirteen, 126-128

Horne, Lena
　Black singer who provided entertainment for Navy men at Camp Robert Smalls during World War II, 78-79

Integration
　See Racial Integration

Kauffold, Lieutenant Vance A., USNR
　An officer who was involved in the training of black naval personnel at Great Lakes, Illinois, during World War II, 110

Kerner, Otto
    Illinois governor in whose cabinet White served in the early 1960s, 116-117

Kidd, USS (DDG-993)
    The Navy got excellent publicity from a Golden Thirteen reunion on board this destroyer in 1982, 48

Knox, Frank
    As Secretary of the Navy, announced in 1942 that blacks would be enlisted in general service ratings but not commissioned as officers, 17-18; Knox's stated policy changed in late 1943 to permit commissioning of black officers, 26-27

Law
    White chose in the 1930s to seek a legal career because it depends on the powers of reasoning, 4; noted lawyers who served as role models, 5-6; White began the practice of law in the late 1930s in Chicago, 7-10; White worked as an assistant U.S. attorney in Chicago from 1939 to 1943, 10-15; highlights of White's post-Navy legal career, 116-119

Lear, Charles B.
    Golden Thirteen member who underwent officer training at Great Lakes, Illinois, and apparently committed suicide shortly after his release from the Navy following World War II, 82, 95-99

Legal Profession
    See Law

Life Magazine
    Published a photo of the Golden Thirteen in an April 1944 issue, 70; published letters to the editor a few weeks after the publication of the photo, 128-129

Marine Corps, U.S.
    Lagged initially behind the Navy in commissioning black officers during World War II but has made considerable progress since then, 49

Martin, Graham E.
    Golden Thirteen member who was quiet, polite, and an excellent football player, 99-101

Mason, USS (DE-529)
    Destroyer escort that was commissioned in World War II with a crew of black enlisted men, 36, 38-40

National Naval Officers Organization
    An association of black naval officers in the Navy of the 1980s, 47-49

Navy Department, Washington, D.C.
   White served as a public information officer for the Navy
   in 1945-46, 41-44, 112-115

Nelson, Dennis D. II
   Golden Thirteen member who underwent officer training in
   1944 at Great Lakes, Illinois, and exhibited a great deal
   of pride in everything he was connected with, 44-45,
   89-90; provided literacy training for black recruits at
   Great Lakes, Illinois, in 1944, 45, 90; disliked
   Commander Daniel W. Armstrong, who oversaw training of
   black Navy men during World War II at Great Lakes, 84-85,
   94

News Media
   White alerted a Chicago reporter when he entered the Navy
   in 1943, 25-26; White worked with newspapers and radio
   stations as a Navy public information officer in 1944-45,
   31-35, 112-113; newspapers near a Navy facility in the
   South were reluctant to cover routine Navy news during
   World War II, 42-43; the Navy got excellent publicity
   from a Golden Thirteen reunion on board the destroyer
   Kidd (DDG-993) in 1982, 48; black newspapers attacked the
   Navy during World War II over its utilization of black
   personnel, 53; Life magazine published a photo of the
   Golden Thirteen in an April 1944 issue, 70; Life
   published letters to the editor a few weeks after the
   publication of the photo, 128-129

Ninth Naval District
   White served as a public information officer at the
   district headquarters at Great Lakes, Illinois, in
   1944-45, 32-35, 86, 94-95, 112

Officer Candidate School
   Members of the Golden Thirteen received officer training
   in segregated Camp Robert Smalls at Great Lakes,
   Illinois, in early 1944, 28-31, 36-37, 45-47, 51, 57-69
   See also Golden Thirteen

Personnel
   Segregated training of enlisted men and officers at Great
   Lakes, Illinois, during World War II, 20-22, 28-31, 36-37
   45-47, 51; manning of the USS Mason (DE-529) with a crew
   of black enlisted men during World War II, 38-39; members
   of largely black ammunition-handling gangs were killed in
   an explosion at Port Chicago, California, in 1944, 39-40;
   concern over effective utilization of personnel near the
   end of World War II, 42; Lester Granger visited a number
   of Navy facilities near the end of World War II to see
   how well the service's policy of integration was being
   implemented, 42-43; black newspapers attacked the Navy
   during World War II over its utilization of black
   personnel, 53; role of the Golden Thirteen in Navy
   recruiting in the 1980s, 125-126

Pinkney, J. B.
  Enlisted Navy man who went through officer training with the Golden Thirteen in early 1944 but was not commissioned, 68-69

Preston, Chief Photographer's Mate Moses, USN
  Served as a photographer at the Great Lakes Naval Training Station during World War II, 34, 79

Public Relations
  White served as a public information officer at Great Lakes, Illinois, in 1944-45, 31-35, 86, 112; White served as a public information officer for the Navy Department in Washington, D.C., in 1945-46, 41-44, 112-115; the Navy got excellent publicity from a Golden Thirteen reunion on board the destroyer Kidd (DDG-993) in 1982, 48; White was asked in 1943 if he could support the Navy's policies when dealing with black newspapers, 53; coverage of visit to Great Lakes by black singer Lena Horne during World War II, 78-79

Racial Integration
  Black and white Navy enlisted men worked together much more toward the end of World War II than they had at the beginning, 34-35, 40; Lester Granger visited a number of Navy facilities near the end of World War II to see how well the service's policy of integration was being implemented, 42-43, 85-88; black naval personnel have achieved a status beyond that accorded blacks in private industry, 49-50

Racial Prejudice
  White calmed black naval personnel who didn't want to obey an order because of the prejudiced attitude of the officer who gave it during World War II, 120-122

Racial Segregation
  Black and white sailors went through segregated boot camps at the Great Lakes Naval Training Station in 1943, 20-22; black officer candidates were trained at segregated Camp Robert Smalls at Great Lakes in early 1944, 28-31, 36-37, 45-47, 51, 57-69; manning of the USS Mason (DE-529) with a crew of black enlisted men during World War II, 38-39; members of largely black ammunition-handling gangs were killed in an explosion at Port Chicago, California, in 1944, 39-40, 86

Reagan, John W.
  Golden Thirteen member who underwent officer training at Great Lakes, Illinois, in early 1944, 80; assessment of, 102-103

Recruiting
  Role of the Golden Thirteen in Navy recruiting in the 1980s, 125-126

Recruit Training
   White went through boot camp at Camp Robert Smalls, Great
   Lakes, Illinois, in 1943, 18-25;   literacy training for
   black recruits at Great Lakes, Illinois, in 1944, 45, 90

Religion
   White has been a member of a number of different
   religious groups, 124

Segregation
   See Racial Segregation

Sheridan, Fort
   See Fort Sheridan, Illinois

Sublett, Frank E.
   Golden Thirteen member who underwent officer training at
   Great Lakes, Illinois, in early 1944 and later became an
   auto repair supervisor and a professional model, 103-104

Training
   White went through boot camp at Camp Robert Smalls, Great
   Lakes, Illinois, in 1943, 18-25; black officer candidates
   were trained at segregated Camp Robert Smalls at Great
   Lakes in early 1944, 28-31, 36-37, 45-47, 51, 57-69;
   literacy training for black recruits at Great Lakes,
   Illinois, in 1944, 45, 90

Unification
   The Navy fought against the formation of a Defense
   Department in the years right after World War II, 41

University of Chicago
   White earned bachelor's degree here in 1935 and law
   degree in 1937, 1, 7

Van Ness, Lieutenant Commander Donald O., USNR (USNA, 1935)
   An officer who was involved in the training of black
   naval personnel at Great Lakes, Illinois, during World
   War II, 110-111

White, William Sylvester
   Birth in 1914, early years in Chicago, and education at
   the University of Chicago, 1, 7; parents of, 1-3, 6, 9,
   122-124; choice of a career in the legal profession, 4;
   role models in the legal profession, 5-6; began the
   practice of law in the late 1930s in Chicago, 7-9; worked
   as an assistant U.S. attorney in Chicago from 1939 to
   1943, 10-15; enlisted in the Navy in 1943 and reported to
   Great Lakes, Illinois, for recruit training, 15-26;
   children of, 19-20, 65, 124-125; unsuccessfully applied
   for a Navy commission prior to entering the service, 27;
   received officer training at Great Lakes, Illinois, in
   early 1944 along with 15 other black enlisted men, 28-31,

36-37, 45-47, 51, 57-69; following his commissioning as an ensign in March 1944, White remained at Great Lakes as a public information officer, 31-35, 86, 112; served as a public information officer for the Navy Department in Washington, D.C., in 1945-46, 41-44, 112-115; made a trip with Lester Granger near the end of World War II to look into the implementation of Navy integration policy, 42-43, 85-88; process of questioning and notification of selection for officer training, 51-55; was nearly appointed to the Illinois Supreme Court in 1988, 116; highlights of post-Navy legal career, 116-119; served in cabinet of Illinois Governor Otto Kerner in the early 1960s, 116-117; White has been a member of a number of different religious groups, 124

Williams, Lewis R.
Close friend of White's who in 1942 was one of the first blacks enlisted in the Navy for a general service rating, 17-18; went through officer training at Great Lakes, Illinois, in early 1944 but was not commissioned, 28-29, 62, 77, 81

www.ingramcontent.com/pod-product-compliance
Lightning Source LLC
Chambersburg PA
CBHW080611170426
43209CB00007B/1405